The Two Red Flags

D0222857

The Two Red Flags is an incisive account of the impact of Socialism on the life and politics of Europe and the former Soviet bloc in the twentieth century. Ranging from Britain and Germany to Italy and Russia, this book covers the origins of Socialism and Communism and their various offshoots in those countries where they had most impact.

The Two Red Flags is an exciting and concise history which provides the reader with a real understanding of the forces at work, and the people who were involved – the roles and personalities of Stalin, Khrushchev, Reagan, Mitterrand, Brandt, Honecker, Wilson and Blair are all considered. Topics discussed include:

- Origins of Socialism, pre-1939
- War and resistance, 1939–45
- Social Democracy and West European recovery, 1945–58
- The Cold War and the Stalinist model, 1945–61
- Democratic Socialists, Communists and the New Left, 1956–68
- The climax of European Social Democracy? 1969–82
- Gorbachev and the collapse of the Soviet Empire, 1989–92
- The resurgence of Social Democracy in the 1990s.

David Childs is Emeritus Professor of Politics at the University of Nottingham and author of *Britain since 1945* (1997).

The Two Red Flags

European Social Democracy and Soviet Communism since 1945

David Childs

London and New York

First published 2000
by Routledge
11 New Fetter Lane, London EC4P 4EE

Simultaneously published in the USA and Canada
by Routledge Inc
29 West 35th Street, New York, NY 10001

© 2000 David Childs

Typeset in Times by Taylor & Francis Books Ltd
Printed and bound in Great Britain by St Edmundsbury, Suffolk

British Library Cataloguing in Publication Data
A catalogue record for this book is available from the British
Library

Library of Congress Cataloging in Publication Data
Childs, David, 1933–
The Two Red Flags: european social democracy and soviet
communism since 1945 / David Childs.
Includes bibliographical references and indexes.
1. Europe–History–1945– 2. Socialism–Europe–History–20th
century. 3. Communism–Soviet Union–History–20th century.
I. Title.
D421.C483 2000
320.53'094'09045–dc21   99–40178
                                                CIP

ISBN 0–415–22195–1 (hbk)
ISBN 0–415–17181–4 (pbk)

Contents

Tables

Abbreviations

AN	Alleanza Nazionale (National Alliance, Italy)
BSP	Bulgarian Socialist Party
CDU	Christlich Demokratische Union (Christian Democratic Union)
CGIL	General Confederation of Italian Labour
CGT	Confédération Générale du Travail (General Confederation of Labour, French Communist-controlled unions)
CIA	Central Intelligence Agency (USA)
CND	Campaign for Nuclear Disarmament (in Britain)
CPGB	Communist Party of Great Britain
CPSU	Communist Party of the Soviet Union
CSU	Christlich Soziale Union (Christian Social Union, in Bavaria)
DA	Demokratischer Aufbruch (Democratic Awakening, East Germany)
DC	Christian Democrats (Italy)
DGB	Deutscher Gewerkschaftsbund (German Trade Union Confederation)
DNA	Norwegian Labour Party
ECSC	European Coal and Steel Community
EEC	European Economic Community
EMU	European Monetary Union
ENA	École Nationale d'Administration
ERM	Exchange Rate Mechanism
ERP	European Recovery Programme (Marshall Aid)
EU	European Union
FDP	Freie Demokratische Partei (Free Democratic Party, Germany)
FI	Forza Italia!

FIDESZ	Alliance of Young Democrats (Hungary)
FN	Front National (France)
FPÖ	Freiheitliche Partei Österreichs (Freedom Party of Austria)
FRG	Federal Republic of Germany (until 1990 just West Germany)
GATT	General Agreement on Trade and Tariffs
GDR	German Democratic Republic (East Germany)
GVP	All-German People's Party
HDF	Hungarian Democratic Forum
ILP	Independent Labour Party (UK)
IMF	International Monetary Fund
KGB	Soviet Security and Intelligence Service, 1954–91
KPD	Kommunistische Partei Deutschlands (Communist Party of Germany)
LRC	Labour Representation Committee
MRF	Movement for Rights and Freedom (Bulgaria)
MRP	Mouvement Républicain Populaire (France)
MSI	Movimento Sociale Italiano (Italian Social Movement)
NATO	North Atlantic Treaty Organisation
NEC	National Executive Committee (of the British Labour Party)
NF	Neues Forum (New Forum)
NPD	Nationaldemokratische Partei Deutschlands (National Democratic Party of Germany)
NUM	National Union of Mineworkers
OEEC	Organization for European Economic Cooperation
OECD	Organisation for European Cooperation and Development
OPEC	Organisation of Petroleum Exporting Countries
ÖVP	Österreichische Volkspartei (Austrian People's Party)
PASOK	Pan-Hellenic Socialist Movement (Greece)
PC	Plaid Cymru (Welsh National Party)
PCE	Partido Comunista de Espana (Communist Party of Spain)
PCF	Parti Communiste Français (French Communist Party)
PCI	Partito Comunista Italiano (Italian Communist Party)
PvdA	Dutch Labour Party
PDS	Partei des Demokratischen Sozialismus (formerly SED, Germany)

PDS	Partito Democratico della Sinistra (Democratic Party of the Left, Italy)
PLO	Palestine Liberation Organization
PS	Parti Socialiste (French Socialist Party)
PSDI	Italian Social Democratic Party
PSI	Partito Socialista Italiano (Italian Socialist Party)
PSIUP	Partito Socialista Italiano di Unità Proletaria (Italian Socialist Party of Proletarian Unity)
PSOE	Partido Socialista Obrero Español (Spanish Socialist Workers' Party)
PSU	Partito Socialista Unificato (Italy)
PSU	Parti Socialiste Unifié (France)
RC	Rifondazione Comunista (Communist Refoundation, Italy)
SAP	Swedish Social Democratic Party
SDP	(East German) Social Democratic Party in 1989
SDP	Social Democratic Party (in Britain)
SED	Sozialistische Einheitspartei Deutschlands (Socialist Unity Party of Germany)
SFIO	Section Française de l'Internationale Ouvrière (French Section of Workers' International, French Socialist Party name before 1970s)
SKDL	Finnish People's Democratic League
SNP	Scottish National Party
SPD	Sozialdemokratische Partei Deutschlands (Social Democratic Party of Germany)
SPÖ	Sozialistische Partei Österreichs (Socialist Party of Austria)
Stasi	State Security Service (of GDR)
SV	Socialist Left Party (Norway)
TUC	Trades Union Congress (Britain)
UDC	Union of Democratic Centre (Italy)
UDF	Union of Democratic Forces (Bulgaria)
UDF	Union pour la Démocratie Française (French centre right umbrella organisation)
UGT	Trade Union Federation (Spain)
UN	United Nations
UNR	Union pour la Nouvelle République
USPD	Unabhängige Sozialdemokratische Partei Deutschlands (Independent Social Democratic Party of Germany)
WEU	Western European Union

Chapter 1

Before 1939

1919: Can the RAF bomb Liverpool, Manchester and Glasgow?

In 1919 Lloyd George, British prime minister, asked the new air force whether it had the capacity to bomb British urban centres such as Liverpool, Manchester and Glasgow. The reason for this frightening request was that Lloyd George and many other members of the establishment feared Britain was on the verge of revolution which, should it break out, could only be suppressed by shock tactics. Thousands of British people had died in German air raids on Britain in the First World War, which had effectively ended on 11 November 1918. As a result bombing was thought to be a practical way of terrorising the masses. The Liberal/Conservative coalition government faced the mutiny of 10,000 British troops at Folkestone in January 1919. Later in the month another 20,000 men at Calais refused to obey orders. Sailors on *HMS Kilbride* hoisted the red flag. In February armed troops demonstrated on Horse Guards Parade, the centre of the government district in London. In Glasgow, Scotland's biggest industrial centre, a general strike was in progress and the red flag flew from the city hall.[1] The normally reliable police had gone on strike in London, Liverpool and other towns.[2] In Ireland death was on the streets as the British government used ruthless methods to crush Michael Collins' IRA rebels who sought independence from Britain. The Labour Party censured the government's policy which had led to the burning of Cork, Balbriggan and other places.[3] In Britain's sprawling Indian Empire the situation was not much better.

1919: 'Someone must act as bloodhound!'

Lloyd George's fears were based not only on what was happening in Britain. The horrors of the First World War had helped to bring down some of the mightiest empires. The first to crash was the Russian Empire. Its fall, in February 1917, was welcomed outside as well as inside Russia. The outgoing tsarist regime had long been detested by democrats the world over. It was at first replaced by a democratic provisional regime until proper elections could be organised. In October this government led by the moderate Socialist lawyer, Alexander Kerensky, was overthrown by Lenin, Trotsky and Stalin, partly by misleading the military wing of the workers' council (Soviet) in Petrograd (St Petersburg). They set up a revolutionary dictatorship, and with it red terror, organised by the Cheka. The Austro-Hungarian Empire followed the tsarist Russian Empire into oblivion on 12 November 1918. The Socialist Karl Renner, also a lawyer, declared the Austrian Republic, thus ending the centuries-old Hapsburg monarchy. The republic suffered from instability and early Leninist/Communist attempts to seize power, their last bloody attempt taking place on 15 June 1919. Among Communist rebels eight died and fifty were wounded.[4]

In neighbouring Germany the Kaiser's regime was overthrown by naval and military mutinies in 1918, and a republic was established. It was headed by Social Democrat Friedrich Ebert, a former saddler and long-time party functionary. It too was subject to attempts by German admirers of Lenin to capture power. They set themselves up as the Communist Party of Germany (Spartacist League) or KPD on 1 January 1919. After they had seized some government buildings, the police headquarters and the Social Democratic newspaper building in Berlin, Ebert asked his friend, Gustav Noske, to take charge of loyal troops and eject them. Noske is reported to have replied, 'Someone must act as bloodhound.'[5] Between 12 and 18 January 1919 bitter fighting took place before the Spartacists were expelled with some tears and more blood. Similar disturbances took place in other German towns.

Far worse was the situation in Hungary, which became independent of Austria as a result of the First World War. There Bela Kun's Communists set up a Soviet-style republic in March 1919. They initiated the red terror before they themselves were engulfed by white terror in the form of Admiral Horthy's legions. Horthy then established a right-wing authoritarian government, which lasted until 1944. Kun sought refuge in Soviet Russia where he fell victim to Stalin in 1939. Even Switzerland, which had been neutral in the war, saw clashes between troops and Socialist demonstrators in 1919.

Socialism in Milwaukee

Something needs to be said about the situation in the USA, a country not usually associated with Socialism. In 1916 the citizens of Milwaukee, Wisconsin, elected the Irish-American Socialist, Daniel Hoan, as their mayor (chief executive). He remained in office for twenty-four years and was elected seven consecutive times.[6] He was not the first Socialist mayor. That honour went to Emil Seidel, elected in 1910.[7] In 1948 a Socialist was elected again, when Frank Zeidler gained office with 124,024 votes to 97,277 for his opponent. He fought three successful campaigns and held office for twelve years. He retired in 1960, having found the strain of office too great.[8] With a population in 1960 of well over 500,000 and a metropolitan area population of over twice that size, Milwaukee was one of America's top industrial cities. Socialist influences came to the city through German and Scandinavian immigrants in the nineteenth century. Although it was something of an exception, Milwaukee was not isolated as a Socialist outpost in the USA. A variety of Socialist groups had come into existence in the last twenty-five years of the nineteenth century across the USA. In 1901 the Socialist Party of America, which officially followed Marxist principles, was established. In 1912 its candidate Eugene V. Debs, an ex-railwayman, gained 897,000 votes in the presidential election – almost 6 per cent of the total and the highest percentage ever gained by a Socialist. In that election, all the candidates leaned to the Left on social issues, stealing some of the Socialists' clothes. Socialist Party membership was around 118,000, and most of those members were American-born.[9] In 1920 Debs attracted 919,799 votes, a lower percentage than in 1912, despite being in prison. The Republican Warren G. Harding won the presidency with 16,152,000 votes to 9,147,353 for his Democratic opponent.[10] What had happened in between? The First World War, which the USA entered in April 1917, brought turmoil into the Socialist camp there as elsewhere. There were splits between those who supported US involvement and those who opposed it. However, Socialist Party (anti-war) candidates did well in municipal elections in that year. In

New York they attracted 22 per cent of the city's voters, in Chicago nearly 34 per cent, in Buffalo over 25 per cent, in Dayton 44 per cent, Toledo 34.8 per cent and Cleveland 19.3 per cent.[11] The government sought to wreck the party. Its offices were raided, many of its leaders, including Debs, were arrested. The US Mail refused to carry its publications. The legal framework of these assaults was the Espionage Act passed in June 1917, which made virtually any kind of opposition to the war illegal.[12] The Bolshevik takeover in Russia further weakened the party, with pro-Leninists eventually founding the Communist Party, and the government cracking down even harder on all kinds of Socialist activity. On May Day 1919 there were riots in American streets: the Communists and the radical Industrial Workers of the World, founded in 1905, joined forces. Most of the Industrial Workers' leaders had been imprisoned for opposition to the war.[13] In July race riots over black housing broke out in Chicago. Postwar living costs had soared, and a wave of strikes hit the USA, which involved railroads, docks, automobile plants and other industries. The Communists attempted to seize control of the unions but were defeated by a movement led by Samuel Gompers, head of the American Federation of Labor (AFofL).[14]

Socialism: 'Free development of each ... condition for free development of all'

The events of 1919 highlight the problems of Socialist movements from their beginnings in the nineteenth century right up to the present time. First, what did they understand by the term 'Socialism'? Second, how were they to achieve their ends? Third, what interim policies would they support in the period before they could start to implement their ideals? Fourth, would they keep themselves in grand isolation or would they be prepared to join coalitions to enable them to introduce specific, limited reforms, or to avoid greater evils? Finally, was Socialism a creed, which appealed to everyone, like Christianity for instance, or was it just for one section of society – the industrial workers, Marx's proletariat?

The labour movements, which had developed in Europe in the wake of nineteenth-century industrialisation, sought, in the first place, to liberate the industrial workers who had few legal, social or political rights. Increasingly they used the French word 'Socialism' to describe their ultimate aim. In France, Pierre Joseph Proudhon believed a Socialist society to be a society where each individual works according to his ability and gets according to his needs. The ideas of Karl Marx, however, came to dominate the working-class movements of Europe, especially those of northern and central Europe. Marx wrote little about the future Socialist/Communist society. He believed he had discovered the laws of motion of capitalist society. Capitalism could produce great wealth but, because the means of producing that wealth were in private ownership, there was a contradiction between production and consumption. The workers (and other employees) could never buy back all they produced. This resulted in surplus production, which, together with the anarchy of the markets, caused slumps leading to ever-greater crises. Experience of these crises would lead the workers to seek an alternative to capitalism, and ultimately they would build a classless society. Marx felt it would be 'unscientific' to try to describe or prescribe in detail how that society would be organised. The key for Marx was to 'expropriate the expropriators' by 'transforming the means of production, land and capital, now chiefly the means of enslaving and exploiting labour, into mere instruments of free and associated labour'.[15] He also believed that after a transitionary period, the length of which would depend on the degree of civilisation in different countries, the state would gradually wither away. For Marx the state was always an instrument of class domination. In capitalist society it was the executive committee of the capitalist class, but in the early stages of the proletarian revolution it would be the instrument of the working class, the dictatorship of the proletariat. As classes faded so would the state: 'In place of the old bourgeois society, with its classes and class antagonisms, we shall have an association, in which the free development of each is the condition for the free development of all.'[16] The 1891 Erfurt Programme of the Social Democratic Party of Germany, the most significant Socialist party in Europe, openly proclaimed Marx's ideas. Only by transforming the capitalist private means of production into property owned by society could misery and repression be ended.[17] The 1901 Vienna Programme of the Social Democratic Workers Party in Austria also closely followed Marx's thinking. It called for the common ownership of the means of production in the hands of 'the people as a whole'.[18]

Founded in 1906, the British Labour Party adopted what was regarded as a Socialist programme in 1918. It called for the common ownership of the means of production, distribution and exchange and their democratic administration. At its national convention in Milwaukee in 1932, the Socialist Party of America called for the transfer of 'the principal industries of the country from private ownership and autocratic management to social ownership and democratic management'.[19] It is interesting in view of later debates that the parties did not advocate state ownership but common ownership. They did not define precisely what they meant by this. According to the German and Austrian programmes, the new society would be democratic and one in which men and women would be treated as equals. The British, American and other Socialist parties were in the forefront of advocating democracy and equality of the sexes. The Austrians were also explicitly anti-racist. This was because the Austro-Hungarian Empire had many nationalities and ethnic groups.

So much for the aim; how was it to be achieved?

1890: 'If only Marx were still by my side'

When Marx and Engels wrote the *Communist Manifesto* (1848) they firmly believed the bourgeoisie could only be overthrown by violent revolution. They were writing in a Europe which was un-democratic and ultimately ruled by force. Over the years until the death of Marx in 1883, they witnessed the success of reform agitation both in extending the franchise and in improving conditions of work. They came to the conclusion that in certain countries the transformation could take place *without* violence. The USA and Britain were among these countries but, despite progress, not Germany. Engels, who died in 1895, lived to see the great successes of the SPD and further advances elsewhere. He also warned against old-style revolutionary attempts to seize power because of the effectiveness of modern weapons in the hands of the state. From their practical experience and for moral reasons, most Socialists sought to achieve their aims by non-violent means. Lenin and his Bolsheviks in Russia were among the few exceptions. Even there, Lenin was opposed by the majority of Socialists, including such leading figures as the father of Russian Marxism, George Plekhanov.

Realising that they could not achieve power overnight, and in accordance with their 'peacefully if we may' strategy, the Socialists developed reform proposals which they hoped would win them more support, improve the lot of their clientele and raise the consciousness of the masses by showing them they could win. Writing in 1890 Engels was thrilled that:

as I write ... the European and American proletariat is reviewing its fighting forces, mobilised under *one* flag, for *one* immediate aim: the standard eight-hour working day, to be established by legal enactment. ... If only Marx were still by my side to see with his own eyes![20]

Of course, Engels was exaggerating. The American Socialists had made big strides but were very much a minority even of the working class, as were Socialists everywhere. Eduard Bernstein, an associate of Engels, and a leading figure in the SPD, set about revising Marx's ideas. He came to the conclusion that the manual working class would never become the 'overwhelming majority', but was likely to decline as the economy became more complex. He believed capitalism could survive its crises. He recognised that the SPD was in fact a reform party aiming at *evolutionary* not *revolutionary* change. It should therefore stop its revolutionary phrase-mongering, which served only to frighten potential supporters. Finally, he believed Socialism was a moral imperative rather than a scientific method. Each generation had a new set of aims to fight for as there never would be a 'final victory'. He met with much hostility within the movement, as many Social Democrats needed the certainty of ultimate victory to sustain them in the years of sacrifice. The biggest Socialist movement was in Germany, where the SPD gained nearly 20 per cent of all votes cast in the parliamentary elections in 1890. They had become the biggest party in Germany. In the last election (1912) before the 'Great War' they gained over 4.25 million votes (34.8 per cent). The second largest party was the Catholic Centre Party with just under 2.04 million votes. The SPD was the largest party in the Reichstag, the German parliament, and would have had more seats had the system been fair.[21] The Danish, Norwegian, Swiss, Swedish and Finnish Socialist parties, set up in 1876–8, 1887, 1888, 1889 and 1899 respectively, followed the German model.

Taking advantage of the Franco-Prussian War, 1870–71, revolutionary groups had seized Paris and set up what became known as the Paris Commune which Marx regarded as the first workers' state. It was soon crushed by French troops and repression followed. As the memories of the Commune began to fade, the authorities relented and in 1879 most of its leaders were pardoned. A complete amnesty was declared in the following year. In this climate the French Workers' Party (POF) was set up by Jules Guesde with

Marx's blessing in 1879. It was also modelled on the SPD. But within three years a schism occurred and the rival Federation of Socialist Workers of France appeared, led by Paul Brousse who was avowedly more reformist. Within the complex web of French left-wing politics a third party was founded, the Parti Socialiste Français, or French Socialist Party. Its leading spirit was Jean Jaurès. Unlike Guesde, he supported participation in coalitions with non-Socialist parties. He modified his stance in order to bring about the merger of his party with Guesde's to form the SFIO in 1905. The SFIO, or French Section of the Workers' International (Section Française de l'Internationale Ouvrière), became the main representative of French Socialism and existed until 1971.[22]

1914: Dogs of war unleashed

On 13 August 1913 August Bebel, the personification of German Social Democracy, died aged 73. He had served as co-chairman of the SPD since 1892 and had been a key figure in the Second International of workers' parties established in 1889.[23] Its first congress in Paris on 14 July 1889, planned to coincide with the centenary of the storming of the Bastille, was attended by around 400 delegates from twenty states, including Germany, France, Austria, Britain and the USA. The congress agreed a long list of practical reforms including the eight-hour working day, no work for children under 14, equality of the sexes and so on. As the American Federation of Labor had decided to hold demonstrations in favour of the eight-hour day on 1 May 1890, the International declared this Labour Day.

Throughout Europe and North America there was labour unrest in the period before the First World War in 1914, and in this the Second International played its part. In the run-up to the First World War there were a number of small wars, such as the crushing of the Boxer Rebellion in China (1898–1900), the Anglo-Boer War (1899–1901), the Russo-Japanese War (1904–5) and the two Balkan wars (1912–13). The International took an honourable stand against imperialism and war, hoping the workers would be able to defeat war fever by strikes in the countries involved. It also sought to replace professional armies by democratically controlled militias. It failed to achieve these noble aims. The untimely death of Bebel, and the assassination of Jaurès in July 1914, at the very time when an SPD delegation was negotiating a common line on the unfolding war with the French Socialists, made it easier for the French and German governments to unleash the dogs of war. The German government presented the war to the German parliament as a war of defence mainly against Russian imperialism. In reality Russia had mobilised its forces (29–30 July) to help its small ally Serbia, which was faced with an impossible ultimatum by Austria-Hungary (28 July). Germany then went to the aid of the Austro-Hungarian Empire, declaring war on Russia (1 August), and France went to the aid of its ally, Russia. The German declaration of war on France came on 3 August. When Germany invaded neutral Belgium (4 August) the British Liberal government lost no time in declaring war on Germany. If the outbreak of war represented a failure for the International, it also revealed the bankruptcy of the existing system. In theory the war should never have happened, given the close family ties between the British, German, Russian and Austrian royal families. But these states were locked into alliances and once the order was given it was difficult to avoid war.

Regarding it as a defensive war against tsarist aggression, the SPD parliamentary group voted for the defence estimates in the Reichstag. It is worth recalling that at that time the majority of parliamentarians belonged to democratic, anti-imperialist parties. The majority of Socialists in other countries also supported their governments, believing they were defending their countries. In France, where Socialists were the second largest group in parliament, two of their members, including Guesde, joined the Government of National Defence. The same happened in neighbouring Belgium, where the Socialists could argue that they simply wanted to defend their country against German invasion. It was no different in Britain, but Ramsay MacDonald,[24] leader of the Parliamentary Labour Party, gave up the leadership because of his opposition to the war. He was replaced by Arthur Henderson, who joined the Liberal-led coalition in May 1915, thus becoming the first Labour cabinet minister. In Germany, Britain, France and elsewhere the Socialists acted as a moderating influence on their governments. As the war intensified, the casualties mounted, and the shortages of food and other consumer goods increased, so did the opposition to the war among the masses. Strikes were common across Europe despite the use of fines, military conscription and imprisonment of strikers. Agitation against the war was also proscribed. In Germany, Rosa Luxemburg and Karl Liebknecht, left-wing Socialists who opposed the war, were among the many imprisoned. They were killed in 1919 by right-wing soldiers. In Britain, the philosopher Bertrand Russell, a Socialist, opposed the war, the mistreatment of conscientious objectors and other abuses. His reward was loss of his lectureship at Trinity College, Cambridge and a six-month spell in prison.[25] In the USA there were more than 200 convictions under the Espionage Act of 1917.[26] In Russia and Serbia the Socialists opposed the war. A number of countries where the Socialist movement was strong – above all the Scandinavian states, Holland, Spain and Switzerland – remained neutral. Their Socialists did not have to make the agonising choices facing their comrades in the belligerent states. They attempted to bring Socialists from these states together, on neutral ground in Zimmerwald (1915), Kienthal (1916) and Stockholm (1917).

Mussolini: 'The greatest lawgiver among living men'

Apart from in Russia, 'law and order' was restored in the European states. 'Law and order' in Eastern Europe, in countries such as Bulgaria, Hungary, Poland, Romania and Yugoslavia, meant nationalistic authoritarian regimes in which Communists and Socialists had no place. To varying degrees they were Fascist in all but name. Italy gave birth to the real thing. Benito Mussolini, the ex-Socialist, created what he called the Fascist Movement, many of whose members were unemployed former soldiers. He used nationalism and fear of Socialism to gain financial and other assistance from the factory owners and big landowners and even from the non-Fascist government. Demobilised officers were given four-fifths of their former pay by the government if they joined the *Fasci di Combattimento*, Mussolini's fighting squads.[27] For the 1921 election the Fascists joined the nationalists and Liberals to form the National Bloc. The Bloc gained 2.2 million votes, the two Socialist parties 2 million, the Catholic *Popolari* 1.4 million, the Democrats and Republicans 822,000 and the Communists 308,000. Having failed to capture parliament, Mussolini staged, with the connivance of the army and the police, his 'March on Rome' in 1922. He was seizing power and over the next few years consolidated what he called his totalitarian state. Winston Churchill, then British Chancellor of Exchequer, commented after meeting Mussolini in 1926 that henceforth no nation would be without an antidote to the bestial appetites of Leninism. In 1933, he pronounced Mussolini the 'greatest lawgiver among living men'.[28]

In Western Europe and the USA most states became more democratic. In the USA and Germany, for instance, although not in France or Switzerland, women got the vote. In Britain women gained suffrage in 1928 on the same basis as men. Many promises were made to the returning servicemen; few were kept. Politically, in most cases, these states were nudged to the left. In Germany, the total left-wing vote remained at about 30 to 40 per cent between 1919 and 1933. The trouble was that the Left was split between the SPD and the KPD, and, for a time, the Independent Social Democrats (USPD). As an alliance with the KPD was out of the question, the SPD could never hope to gain a parliamentary majority. Only through coalitions with right of centre parties like the (Catholic) Centre Party could it gain office. A similar situation existed throughout Western Europe due to the split between the democratic Socialists and the Communists. Also in most countries a proportion of the industrial workers voted for parties which had the backing of the Catholic Church. Third, the expectation that the workers would become the overwhelming majority of the voters had nowhere been realised. Finally, the fact that the electoral systems were based on proportional representation made one-party majorities virtually impossible. In Britain, where blue-collar workers formed a majority, Labour found it difficult to gain a majority even though the electoral system of 'first past the post' made this easier in theory. Nevertheless, in 1924 the first Labour government held office for a few months under Ramsay MacDonald. In the postwar elections Labour's vote increased to 22.2 per cent in 1918, 29.5 per cent in 1922, 30.5 per cent in 1923, 33 per cent in 1924 and 37.1 per cent in 1929. Driven out of office by the Conservative 'Red letter scare' of 1924, MacDonald formed his second minority government in 1929. With world capitalism 'stabilised', it looked as though, at least in Western Europe, Social Democrats could gradually tilt their countries towards the beginning of Socialism. Capitalism during this period did not produce full employment anywhere and great poverty existed, but far worse was to come.

1929: 'A ... headlong rush to sell'

The day of 24 October 1929 became known as Dark Thursday in the USA. The stock market had been weak for some days before, but on that day 'there was a great unrestrained and unexplained headlong rush to sell'.[29] The Great Depression had started. Overnight stocks and shares became worthless. Some former millionaires went broke, a few killed themselves. It was the same in Berlin, London, Vienna and elsewhere. Business confidence had been shaken and American loans to Europe were recalled. In Austria the biggest bank, the Rothschild-owned Creditanstalt, collapsed in May 1931. Large and small firms were threatened by the collapse, a coup was attempted, the government fell, the Austrian state itself faced bankruptcy. It was saddled with debts from the peace settlement. On 20 May 1932 a government led by Dr Engelbert Dollfuß of the Christian Social Party was formed; it had a one-vote majority in parliament.[30]

In Germany the developing world economic crisis produced growing governmental instability and mounting unemployment. The various strands of democratic politics could not come together to solve the crisis. The Nazis blamed it on the 'system', on Jewish bankers such as Rothschild. In the election of 1930 the Nazi vote increased from 2.6 per cent to 18.3 per cent. Thus the Nazis were second only to the SPD with 24.5 per cent. The KPD vote also increased from 10.6 to 13.1 per cent. In the summer election of 1932 the Nazis became the biggest party, with 37.4 per cent to 21.6 per cent for the SPD and 14.6 per cent for the KPD. The Centre Party collected 12.5 per cent. The Nazis had attracted previous non-voters and had squeezed the largely Protestant right and centre right parties. In November 1932, in the last fully free elections, which had a lower turnout, the Nazi vote slipped back to 33.1 per cent, the SPD to 20.4 per cent, the Centre to 11.7 per cent, but the KPD rose to 16.8 per cent. The militarist/monarchist German National People's Party (DNVP) increased its vote from 5.9 to 8.8 per cent. Hating the Social Democrats and fearing the Communists more than they despised the Nazis, the old right-wing politicians persuaded the president, ex-Field Marshal Hindenburg, to appoint Hitler Chancellor on 30 January 1933.

Hitler was head of a government in which the Nazis were in a minority. He had no majority in the Reichstag. He needed a dramatic event to turn the tide. On 20 February it was announced that the Reichstag had been set on fire as the prelude to a KPD coup. Hindenburg sanctioned the suspension of civil rights and Communism, and some SPD officials and others were arrested. Elections were then held on 5 March with the Nazi SA stormtroopers patrolling the streets as auxiliary police. Opposition meetings were broken up and leftist papers banned. On a high turnout of 88.7 per cent the Nazis gained 43.9 per cent and their allies, the DNVP, 8 per cent. The SPD vote was 18.3 per cent, the KPD 12.3 per cent and the Centre 11.2 per cent. Four other parties gained 4.7 per cent. The Communists were not allowed to take their seats and Hitler, with threats and promises, got the Reichstag to give his government power for four years. Only the SPD voted against him. Thus Hitler had his dictatorship. Many leading Communists fled to Soviet Russia but Stalin distrusted them and killed more of them than Hitler did.[31] In Austria, Dollfuß used events in Germany to justify the setting up of a Fascist-style regime. He was backed by Mussolini, not yet an ally of Hitler. The armed resistance of the Austrian Socialists in 1934 was crushed with heavy loss of life.[32]

1931: 'Bolshevism run mad'

In Britain the economic crisis brought about the fall of the Labour government, the members of which could not agree on what measures to take to solve it. MacDonald and Chancellor of the Exchequer Philip Snowden were prepared to take the Treasury line and cut the already meagre social welfare payments. Most of the government opposed this. King George V then asked MacDonald to form a national unity government. He did so, and he and his supporters were expelled from the Labour Party. Cuts followed in public sector pay, social benefits and other public spending. The navy mutinied at its base in Invergordon in Scotland. In the election which followed, Snowden claimed the Labour programme was 'Bolshevism run mad'.[33] MacDonald's national government, based mainly on the Conservatives, gained a massive majority with a vote of 67 per cent. Labour polled 30.6 per cent and the Independent Liberals 0.5 per cent. In both Germany and Britain the economic crisis and fear of Communism had led to strong right-wing governments. In the establishment there was some sympathy for Fascism, with Lord Rothermere's *Daily Mail* in the vanguard. But the establishment had no need of extreme measures; they were secure with their democratic dictatorship in parliament. Oswald Mosley's Fascism was irrelevant.

In France the Socialists and (left-Liberal) Radicals formed a government after their electoral victory in 1932 but, like their British comrades, could not agree on a policy to beat the slump. Their ministry foundered after introducing orthodox financial measures: 'The whole policy amounted to a direct attack on the interests of the electoral clientele which had voted the government into office.'[34] France also faced a Fascist onslaught. On 6 February 1934 right-wing leagues, L'Action Française, Croix de Feu and others, fought the police for six hours to get control of the approaches to the Chamber of Deputies, the French parliament. They failed, but not before fourteen of them had died and over 200 had been seriously injured. The police suffered one fatality and nearly one hundred injured.[35] Their agitation collapsed after the government resigned and was replaced by a more centrist cabinet. The fury of the Right had been unleashed by a financial scandal involving the Jewish financier Stavisky, who had floated worthless bonds. They alleged the government had sought to hush up the affair, even have him murdered, to shield influential individuals.

Hendrik de Man and Ernst Wigforss

The slump revealed the fact that Europe's Socialists had no specific plan to deal with crises within capitalism. As for the Communists, all they could advocate was the Soviet system. They openly called for a *Soviet* Britain, a *Soviet* Germany, a *Soviet* France and so on. This gave ammunition to their opponents and stoked the fears of those who believed they were a conspiracy. Despite denials, the Communists did receive funds from Moscow, and orders from the Communist International, Comintern. Mussolini and Hitler did not really have an answer either. In Italy the banks were on the verge of crashing and were only saved by nationalisation. In Germany Hitler intensified traditional German intervention policies – road building, salary and price control, subsidies for firms replacing imports, help for agriculture, control of capital exports, control of imports, encouragement for new technologies, and later, rearmament. Marxists such as John Strachey believed there was little difference between what Hitler was doing and Roosevelt's New Deal in America. Both took office in 1933. Although strictly a democrat, in fact a Liberal, Keynes advocated something similar in Britain. Labour politicians preached a vague mixture of Keynesianism and Soviet-style central planning. In Belgium the Socialists adopted Hendrik de Man's 1933 *Plan van den Arbeid*, which had similarities to Keynesianism. All these ideas involved 'class collaboration' in that they involved trade unions, employers and governments working together to their mutual benefit.[36] Where they gained office, in the Scandinavian states, Social Democratic governments embarked upon interventionist and welfare policies.

In 1924 the Danish Social Democrats formed their first government, but its term of office was short. In 1929 the Social Democrats formed their second government, this time with the Social Liberals, and they remained in coalition until 1940. They imposed rigorous exchange controls, helped agriculture and promoted employment. In 1933 they adopted the Social Reform, which revised and consolidated social legislation, making Denmark a pioneer in providing social security for the general population. A new Education Act (1937) modernised and developed primary schools, especially in rural areas.[37] In Sweden the Social Democrats (SAP) became the largest party in 1917. They were in and out of office in the 1920s. Under the influence of Ernst Wigforss and Per Albin Hansson (leader 1926–46), the SAP advocated a massive reflationary policy of government-sponsored public works and deficit spending. A deal with the Agrarians in 1933 enabled the SAP government to put this into practice in return for subsidies to agriculture. By the summer of 1936 the total number of unemployed had fallen from 139,000 (in 1933) to 21,000.[38] The SAP was on course to remain in office until 1976. The most left-wing of the Scandinavian Social Democratic parties, the Norwegian Labour Party, dropped the dictatorship of the proletariat from its programme in 1927 and gradually lined up with its more reformist neighbours. In 1935 it too formed a coalition similar to the coalition in Sweden. Social Democracy had been the main force in Finland before the Russian revolution. After it, the split of 1918 occurred and the Communist Party was banned. The reformist Social Democrats, led by V. Tanner, took part in government most of the time. It is easy to underrate the achievements of the Scandinavian Social Democrats in securing an extended period of office due to their alignment with the agrarian parties. In the rest of Europe this proved impossible and made the rise of Fascism that much easier.[39]

1936: 'Our investments ... no trouble' with Franco

The rise of Fascism and then Nazism was increasingly seen as a challenge to the democracies and above all to the Left. Stalin changed the policy of the Comintern in 1935 to one of seeking a broad 'People's Front' against Fascism. Such fronts would encompass individuals of all shades of opinion, not just Communists and Socialists. In France the strategy led to victory of the Popular Front of (left-Liberal) Radicals, the SFIO and the Communists in 1936. SFIO leader Leon Blum headed the new government formed on 4 June. Earlier, in February, in neighbouring Spain, the Popular Front had won a narrow victory. It was even less united than its French counterpart, being made up of anarchists and Catalan separatists, as well as leftist Republicans, Socialists[40] and Communists. A group of generals, under Francisco Franco's leadership, raised the standard of revolt in July against the Republican government. The Nationalists, as the generals called their alliance, were a motley group of monarchists, Catholics and (Fascist) Falangists. They made widespread use of Moorish troops from Spanish Morocco, but their victory in March 1939 was secured by assistance from Nazi Germany and Fascist Italy.[41] The democracies pursued a policy of 'non-intervention', depriving the Republic of the right to purchase war materials. They claimed they feared an escalation of the conflict if foreign powers competed in selling arms. In fact, the British and Americans were influenced by commercial interests and by harrowing reports of mob violence. Claude G. Bowers, US Ambassador, commented, 'our investments ... the Telephone Company, the International Banking Corporation, the General Electric, the General Motors, and the Ford plants ... should have no trouble with the new [Nationalist] regime'.[42] Non-intervention forced the Republic into the arms of Stalin's Soviet Union, which sent weapons and advisers. The Comintern recruited men from many states, including the USA, to fight for the Republic in the International Brigades, which were largely under Communist control. From being a very small party in 1936, the Communists gradually got more and more influence. Internal divisions on the Republican side undermined its power to resist. The Nationalists were under the strict discipline imposed by Franco.

The war became a great romantic cause for the Left. Political tourists, such as American writer Ernest Hemingway and British Labour leader Clement Attlee, flocked to Madrid. But the war also caused problems. The British Conservative government and Blum's Popular Front government agreed on non-intervention. British Labour and European Social Democratic politicians did not wish to become embroiled with the Communists yet they did not want to be seen leaving the Republic in the lurch. It was very much a media war with horror stories on both sides.[43] The European Left had to face the fact that Stalin's secret policemen and their helpers were murdering left-wing rivals, claiming they were Franco spies. Many chose to believe Stalin. In Britain the Independent Labour Party (ILP), which had broken away from the Labour Party in 1932, campaigned against Stalinist crimes including the Moscow trials of leading Communists whom Stalin distrusted.[44] George Orwell attempted to set the record straight on Spain in his *Homage To Catalonia.*

The Soviet Union became very popular in the 1930s. Its leader Joseph Stalin claimed the Soviet planning system had abolished unemployment and was producing unprecedented economic growth. Racism was banned and sexual equality was being achieved. Collective farming was transforming village life. The constitution of 1936 was 'the most democratic in the world'. These claims were publicised by an international army of 'fellow travellers'.[45] Among them were writers Theodore Dreiser (USA), André Gide (France), the 'Red Dean' of Canterbury, Dr Hewlett Johnson, the scientist J.D. Bernal, and the Fabians Sidney and Beatrice Webb (Britain). While resolutely resisting Communist attempts at affiliation, the Labour Party urged Neville Chamberlain's British government to seek an alliance with the Soviet Union to resist Fascism and above all Hitler's expansionism. Chamberlain was cool and preferred to appease Hitler when he remilitarised the Rhineland (1936), seized Austria (1938), and got Britain and France to agree, at the Munich Conference, to Germany taking the Sudetenland from Czechoslovakia (1938). Admiration for the Soviet Union cooled dramatically when the Hitler–Stalin Pact was announced in August 1939. The Second World War followed days later.[46]

Chapter 2

War and resistance
1939–45

1939: 'Life went on much as usual'

Clement Attlee, the British Labour leader, recovering from an operation, was playing a leisurely game of golf in North Wales on 3
September 1939, when he heard the news that Britain had declared
war on Germany. It is not recorded whether he continued.[1] His
parliamentary colleague, young Welsh firebrand Aneurin Bevan,
greeted the news by playing Spanish Republican marching songs on
his gramophone.[2] Young German Social Democrat Willy Brandt,
exiled in Norway, was on stand-by editorial duty at the Norwegian
socialist paper *Arbeiderbladet* on that day. Over the radio he heard
British Prime Minister Neville Chamberlain announce that a 'state
of war' existed with Germany because Hitler had failed to respond
to the British ultimatum to withdraw from Poland, which had been
invaded by German forces two days earlier. Brandt was astonished
at how casually his superiors took the announcement.[3] They had
become used to the appeasement of Nazi Germany by Britain and
France, and were too shaken by the Hitler–Stalin Pact to expect any
decisive action. In neutral Norway, and in most other places in
Europe, 'Life went on much as usual'[4] from September 1939 to
April 1940. This was the period of the 'phoney war' when there was
little military activity.

The main Labour and Social Democratic parties had concluded
that Britain and France were right to declare war on Germany,
though most of them hoped their countries would not become
embroiled in the conflict. The exiled SPD also supported the
democracies against Nazi Germany. At first the Communist parties
took the same line. Their position soon changed on orders from
Moscow in accordance with the Hitler–Stalin Pact.[5] In France the

party was banned and many of its leaders were interned. In Britain it was allowed to continue although its organ, *The Daily Worker*, was banned in 1940. The British Labour Party agreed to a political truce for the duration of the war but refused to join the Chamberlain-led government. The small ILP opposed the war throughout as imperialist. The Soviet attack on Finland in 1939 nearly resulted in the democracies being at war with the Soviet Union, for they gave support to democratic Finland. However, after stiff resistance, Finland had to agree to Soviet peace terms and ceded considerable areas of territory.

Hitler brought the phoney war to an end by lightning strikes – directed first against Denmark and Norway on 9 April 1940. In Denmark there was little immediate resistance. The Germans promised to respect Denmark's independence and integrity and the Social Democratic–Radical Liberal government, first elected in 1929, remained in office.[6] The two main opposition parties joined it. The government was forced, however, to accede to the Anti-Comintern Pact, which entailed no obligations outside Denmark but did require it to ban the Danish Communist Party. In Norway there was heavy fighting, after which the king and coalition government sought safety in Britain. Hitler's Blitzkrieg struck Belgium, Holland, Luxembourg and France in May 1940, leading to their early capitulation. The governments of Belgium and Holland sought sanctuary in Britain from where they encouraged resistance. In France the situation was far more complicated.

The fall of Norway sealed the fate of British Prime Minister Chamberlain. He was held responsible for the failure of the British expedition to Norway. Despite much criticism in parliament, he survived a censure motion but decided to go. With the support of the Labour Party, Churchill formed a government on 10 May 1940. Attlee and the Labour deputy leader, Arthur Greenwood, joined the five-member War Cabinet. Other Labour members and Liberals joined their Conservative colleagues in the broad coalition government. Thus Britain faced the problems of the fall of France and the coming Battle of Britain more united than ever.

Most Germans living in France aged between 17 and 55 were interned, including many anti-Nazis such as Social Democrats Rudolf Breitscheid, Rudolf Hilferding and Erich Ollenhauer. Breitscheid, formerly chairman of the SPD parliamentary group, and Hilferding, a former German finance minister, were among those handed over by the Vichy regime to the Gestapo. Both died in captivity. Ollenhauer, future chairman of the SPD, managed, with the aid of William Gillies, International Secretary of the Labour Party, to reach London from neutral Portugal.[7] Ollenhauer arrived in England on 15 January 1941, by which time the position of German refugees there had improved. In Britain too panic and prejudice had led to the internment of 'enemy aliens'. Between 25,000 and 30,000 refugees from Nazism were interned in 1940. Due to the intervention of the Labour Party and TUC many of them were released in early 1941.[8]

After the fall of France in June 1940 the democratic republic was replaced by Marshal Pétain's Vichy regime. Those who had opposed the transfer of power to the pro-German First World War hero were arrested, among them Socialist Leon Blum. Only a minority of Blum's comrades agreed with him.[9] Later, however, Blum committed the Democratic Socialists to General de Gaulle's Free French movement.[10] Many French people thought Pétain represented the only chance for France to survive. The new regime enjoyed international recognition. Three-fifths of French territory, including Paris, were occupied. But the vast French Empire and the fleet remained under Vichy control. The Communists continued their policy of being tacit allies[11] of the Nazis, denouncing the British and De Gaulle, and seeking fraternisation with the Germany army. They were lucky that the occupiers did not restore their legality and that Pétain maintained his opposition to them, arresting Communist activists.[12]

1941: 'Our ... ever deceitful enemy'

Hitler attacked the Soviet Union on 22 June 1941, and later that month Finland, Italy, Romania and Hungary followed. Social Democratic-led Finland was determined to recover the territory lost in 1940. The Social Democratic Speaker of the Finnish parliament summed up what many of his people thought: 'We are not alone ... the German nation is now crushing with its steel army our traditional, ever treacherous and ever deceitful enemy.'[13] Finland avoided going to war with the Western Allies. The Nazi invasion of the Soviet Union not only brought in a new and powerful opponent of Nazism and Fascism, it also unleashed resistance movements throughout Europe.

The Communist parties abruptly changed their line and called for resistance to the Nazis. They were illegal throughout Europe – apart, that is, from in neutral Sweden and Switzerland, and in

Britain. This illegality was an advantage in that they had gained long experience of working in the shadows. In France the Communists started their resistance activities by choosing soft targets – individual members of the German armed forces. This led to German reprisals, often against Jews, and served little military purpose. Everywhere the British and Americans sent supplies to the resistance groups, Communist and non-Communist alike. The Communists often proved more militant. From London, De Gaulle co-ordinated the French resistance, forming it into the National Council of the Resistance. Particularly important in France was the sabotage of railways up to the D-Day landings. Helping Allied aircrew escape was also important. In southern France, Greece, Italy and Yugoslavia civil war conditions prevailed, with resistance armies opposing the Germans and their allies, the native Fascist militias. In Belgium, Holland and Norway the Socialists remained the key political force in the underground. The Communists, however, were helped by their militancy and by the growing prestige of the Soviet Union resulting from the success of the Red Army. Everywhere military experts had been sceptical about the Red Army's ability to withstand the Nazi war machine. Yet in February 1943 the Germans faced their first, decisive, military defeat (an even greater psychological defeat) when the remnants of the Sixth Army surrendered at Stalingrad. Everywhere the Communists gained more supporters. In Britain, for example, by late 1943 Communist Party membership 'had risen to a little over 55,000, a tripling, or possibly quintupling, in only thirty months'.[14] Another factor aided the resistance movements. This was the increasing conscription of labour throughout occupied Europe to work in Germany. Many chose to join the resistance in preference to life as a forced labourer in the Third Reich or as a conscript soldier in one of the Fascist armies. As the tide of war turned against Germany, more sought to join the winning side.

On 5 March 1943 workers in the northern Italian city of Turin went on strike. The Allied invasion of southern Italy began on 10 July. King Victor Emmanuel, seeing the writing on the wall, then took action to remove Mussolini, in an attempt to save his monarchy and the traditional order. In his place as head of government he appointed Marshal Badoglio. When strikes and demonstrations broke out against the war, the authorities used force to suppress them. Confusion followed. Eventually Emmanuel negotiated an armistice 'amounting to a virtual surrender'[15] with the Allies, which was announced on 8 September – but the Germans struck back. They occupied most of the country. They rescued Mussolini and set him up as head of a puppet state, the Italian Social Republic, at the small resort of Salò in northern Italy. From the armistice to the final capitulation of the German forces in Italy in May 1945, the Italians were subject to major armies fighting across their land, and to increasing civil war. Emmanuel's government and the Mussolini state both claimed their loyalties. In October 1943 Emmanuel's government declared war on Nazi Germany. The king's government was backed by all the non-Fascist parties, and at first they worked together in a grand coalition. It soon became clear, however, that the Communists (PCI) and the new Christian Democratic Party (DC) would be the decisive forces in postwar Italy. Pietro Nenni's Socialists (PSIUP) used more left-wing rhetoric than the Communists, but were weaker on the ground. As elsewhere, the Communists benefited from the prestige of Soviet arms, their militancy and good underground organisation. Back from Moscow, PCI leader Palmiro Togliatti was not calling for a Communist takeover. Stalin's line was still supporting the 'anti-Hitler coalition'. Out of deference to the Western powers he had dissolved the Comintern in 1943. There was to be no talk of Socialism. In any case, Churchill sought to maintain or restore the old order in Italy. Doubtless he worried as the Italian partisans, often Communist-led, fought pitched battles with the Germans. They played a major role in liberating Florence in August 1944.[16] The Nazis took savage reprisals. In April 1945 open insurrection broke out in the main northern industrial centres of Genoa, Turin and Milan. Heavy fighting followed before the Germans either surrendered or withdrew. Communist partisans eventually caught and shot Mussolini.

1945–6: 'We are the masters now'

Throughout Europe the prewar order was in question. Many, whatever their social position, felt the prewar elites had failed. In many cases they had collaborated with the Nazi occupation or even advocated Fascism. There was widespread feeling that, after so many wartime sacrifices, there should be no return to the unemployment, poverty and hierarchy which had prevailed in the 1930s. Everywhere the Left increased its prestige because of its part in the resistance. Elections revealed this.

In 1944 in Sweden the Communists captured 10.3 per cent of the vote. In 1945 in Denmark they gained 12.5 per cent of the vote, in Norway 11.9 per cent, and in Finland 23.5 per cent. Of course in all those states the Socialist/Social Democrats remained the main force on the Left. The same was true in Belgium and Holland, where in 1946 the Communists scored 12.7 and 10.6 per cent respectively.

In France in October 1945 the Communists with 25 per cent and the Socialists with 23 per cent came near to winning an absolute majority. The Radicals scored 10 per cent. The old Popular Front parties had achieved a decisive victory. The traditional Right achieved a mere 16 per cent. However, there was a new force in the field. The Catholic Church and De Gaulle supported the Mouvement Républicain Populaire (MRP), which presented itself as a moderate, all-class movement. Fearing the Left, the Vatican was encouraging the formation of such groups throughout Europe. In a referendum on 2 June 1946, the majority of Italians voted for a republic. But on the same day, in the first free elections for over twenty years, the DC, backed by the Catholic Church, emerged as the biggest single party with 35.2 per cent of the vote. The PCI gained 19 per cent, but the PSIUP scored 20.7 per cent. In neighbouring Austria it was a similar story. The Church-backed People's Party came out ahead of the rival Socialist Party. The Catholic Church had succeeded in repackaging traditional Catholic parties to appear modern, moderate, people's parties. However, in most Western European countries, coalition governments were formed which usually included, or in most cases were led by, Socialists. In Britain Labour got its first Commons majority in July 1945. Many thought Socialism, in one form or another, was sweeping through Europe. As Sir Hartley Shawcross, the Attorney-General in Attlee's Labour government, put it (2 April 1946) in the Commons, 'We are the masters at the moment, and not only at the moment, but for a very long time to come.'

Chapter 3

Social Democracy and West European recovery 1945–58

1945: 'Socialist ... and proud of it'

A general swing to the Left was awaited by many after the Second World War, but among the surprises was the success of Labour in Britain in July 1945, and the failure of the SPD in Germany. Although wartime polls and by-elections indicated a leftward movement, Churchill's prestige was such that few thought he could be defeated. Under a variety of labels, the Conservatives polled 9.96 million votes. The total opposition vote was over 15 million. Labour gained 11.99 million and the Liberals 2.24 million. Other parties considered more left wing than Labour – Common Wealth, the Communist Party and the ILP – standing in a very small number of constituencies attracted 260,000 votes. Also left-wing were the Scottish Nationalists (30,595), the Welsh Nationalists (14,751) and the Irish Nationalists in Northern Ireland (148,078).[1] The figures alone do not fully bring out the extent of the 'Left's' victory. Turnout was 72.7 per cent, that is higher than in the previous election (71.2 per cent in 1935) but lower than in 1931, 1929 or 1924. The election registers were out of date and considerable numbers of new voters found they were not registered. Much has been made of the service vote, but many servicemen did not get the chance to vote partly because the war against Japan was still in progress. Many older people, including women and the middle class, voted Labour for the first time.

Labour's victory had been won on a policy of moderate nationalisation, welfare and housing improvements, and support for the new United Nations and Britain's allies. The rhetoric of Socialism had been used. Speaking for Labour's executive committee, Emmanuel Shinwell, soon to be one of Attlee's ministers, thrilled the Labour conference in December 1944:

If we are accused of being Socialists, if we are accused of inter-
fering with free enterprise, our answer is, 'Yes, we are Socialists,
and we intend to abolish the specious and spurious free enterprise which impinges upon the liberty of the working class and
makes profit for the few.'

Labour's election programme, *Let Us Face The Future*, proclaimed,
'The Labour Party is a socialist party and proud of it.' In office
Labour carried through its basic election pledges by nationalising
the Bank of England, civil aviation, coal mines, electricity, gas, iron
and steel, and public transport, including the docks, inland water-
ways, London transport, railways, road haulage and road passenger
transport. Altogether, the nationalised industries employed 10 per
cent of the labour force or 2.3 million people.[2] For the workers,
especially the miners, one should not underestimate the importance
of the nationalisation measures. For them, nationalisation was the
acid test of whether Labour was serious about its principles.
However, it can be argued that the significance of these moves was
greatly overestimated at the time by Labour and its opponents.
Most of the nationalised industries were natural monopolies
already subject to public control and, in some cases, local authority
ownership. Most were problem industries which suffered from long-
term decline. When the price of electricity, gas or rail fares went up
the government got the blame. The Conservatives did not object
fundamentally to most of the nationalisation programme.[3] Of
greater long-term benefit to Labour's own constituency was the
establishment of the National Health Service (NHS) along with
improvements in social welfare provision. Although various
improvements had been agreed by the wartime coalition, there is no
certainty that had the Conservatives been re-elected they would
have legislated in this direction. The question will continue to be
asked whether Labour could have done more to make Britain a
more modern and 'classless' society by abolishing the Lords, ending
the divisive school system and implementing other measures. For
Attlee these were not issues.[4]

Labour's most dramatic move abroad was implementing independence for India, Pakistan, Ceylon (Sri Lanka) and Burma. Britain
had made vague declarations of its intention to free its Indian
Empire for decades. During the war, negotiations with the Congress,
India's main political party, had broken down, and its leaders,
including Gandhi, had been imprisoned. Had Attlee's government

resisted independence, it would have been faced with colonial upheavals on a colossal scale, but that threat does not detract from its decision to make a speedy withdrawal. France and Holland were prepared to fight colonial wars, which they lost, before agreeing to the independence of their colonies. Churchill bitterly opposed independence for the Indian Empire.[5]

In foreign policy terms, the greatest shock for Labour MPs and activists was the rapid deterioration in relations with the Soviet Union and the subsequent Cold War. Labour members had been dismayed that British troops had been used to prevent Athens falling into the hands of the Communist-led Greek resistance EAM/ELAS in December 1944. Attlee, still in coalition with Churchill, claimed Britain was simply conducting relief operations and establishing conditions in which the Greeks could make a free choice.[6] In reality, neither side was without warts, and British motives were driven by fear of Soviet control of the eastern Mediterranean. British troops, aided by Japanese units, were to be used again and again to re-establish colonial regimes in Asia once Attlee was premier and the Japanese had surrendered. Much greater disappointment was to come for Labour as it became ever more difficult for the Western powers to work with Stalin. He seemed determined to extend the Soviet Empire as far as he could by any means short of a general war. Many on the Left sympathised with the Soviet Union because of its appalling sacrifices in the common cause and were inclined to overlook Stalin's crimes in Germany and Central and Eastern Europe. Reports of earlier atrocities, such as the murder of the Polish officers in the Katyn Woods, were dismissed as 'Fascist propaganda',[7] as was the appalling behaviour of Soviet troops in Germany. But the Labour government could not ignore the fact that an 'iron curtain', as Churchill put it, was descending across Europe.[8]

1948: 'What would become of Germany was still a mystery'

On 1 July 1948 Willy Brandt became a German citizen again. He had given up his Norwegian nationality and a secure job as a journalist for the Norwegian Socialist movement to take up work in Berlin for the SPD. As he later wrote about that time, 'What would become of Germany was still a mystery.'[9] Much of prewar Germany had been incorporated into Poland or the Soviet Union.

Millions of Germans had been driven from their homes. The rest of Germany had been divided into four zones of occupation – US, British, French and Soviet. Berlin, in the middle of the Soviet Zone, was divided into four sectors. Although at Potsdam in July 1945 the leaders of the USA (Truman), Soviet Union (Stalin) and Britain (Churchill and then Attlee) had agreed to run Germany as an economic whole, the Soviet Zone had been effectively separated from the three Western Zones by Stalin. Partly because of the relative poverty of Britain and France, the three Western zones were merged under effective US leadership. Local and regional elections were held, and democratic political life re-emerged with the Christian Democrats and the SPD as the two main parties. In the Soviet Zone the Nazi dictatorship had been replaced by a Soviet one, with local Communists carrying out the orders of the Soviet Military Administration. From West Germany, Kurt Schumacher, leader of the SPD in the three Western zones, attempted to save his comrades and their party in the Soviet Zone. As is discussed in the next chapter, despite his efforts they were forced into a merger with the Communists in 1946.

1952: Britain's future, 'little more than a German satellite'

Schumacher was a heroic figure.[10] Pale and gaunt, he had been wounded in the First World War and suffered in Hitler's concentration camps. He was from East Prussia, part of the lost territories, and a member of the Reichstag until 1933. He strongly opposed any alliance, let alone a merger, with the KPD. He argued that if the Communists had become democrats and wanted a 'German road to Socialism' instead of a Soviet one, they should disband their party and join the SPD. For the Nazis he had been a hate figure and he was equally one for the Communists. He led the party in West Germany and tried to keep an underground SPD alive in the Soviet Zone. He died a disappointed man in 1952.

The Americans had soon come to understand that the German economy was the key to prosperity in Western Europe and that if there was no prosperity either the Communists or a new rightist movement would gain power. They therefore invited the states of Europe to band together in the European Recovery Programme (ERP). This was announced by US Secretary of State George Marshall in 1947. Stalin rejected 'Marshall Aid', regarding it as interference. The states in the Soviet sphere were forced to follow. ERP ran from 1948 and played a major part in assisting economic revival. In Germany, the new currency, the Deutsche Mark, was introduced in 1948, replacing the failing Reichsmark. In an effort to prevent its introduction in Berlin and, if possible, drive the Western Allies out of West Berlin, Stalin imposed a blockade against the Western sectors of the city. A military showdown looked increasingly likely. The Western powers avoided further confrontations with the Soviets by airlifting food, medical supplies and fuel into the beleaguered city. From June 1948 to May 1949 they fed the two million inhabitants of West Berlin via the airlift. Seeing he could not win, Stalin climbed down. The new currency was a sign of hope throughout West Germany despite widespread poverty and unemployment. Increasingly, the Western Allies lifted the restrictions they had imposed on the German economy in 1945. The Germans responded to the challenge and by the early 1950s West Germany was forging ahead. It must be pointed out that Germany benefited from the demand created by the Korean War, 1950–3, which led to an unsustainable rearmament programme in Britain and opened a gap in world markets.[11] The responsible attitude of the German trade unions (DGB) was another important factor.[12] The massive influx of refugees helped to keep wages relatively low. Adenauer, under pressure, agreed to maintain the *Mitbestimmung* or co-determination policies demanded by the DGB and introduced by the Allies. A generous welfare package, based on the Swedish model, was also introduced. By 1952 the young British Labour MP Tony Crosland told his friend, former Chancellor Hugh Dalton, after a trip to Germany, that things were going ahead fast in West Germany and that Britain in future would be 'little more than a German satellite'.[13]

The German 'miracle' was repeated in Belgium, the Netherlands, France, Italy and the Scandinavian states. It was based on replacing war losses, technological innovation, cheap raw material imports, the growing use of credit and, not least, rearmament. It meant full employment and rapidly growing standards of living. It was the classic age of the 'mixed economy'. It was a period when trade unions could demand more for their members. Where Social Democrats controlled the unions – in Germany, Scandinavia and Austria – there were fewer days lost in industrial disputes (see Table 3.1). This 'golden age' came to an end with the first oil crisis of 1973. Since then the long-term tendency has been for unemployment to rise. In

Table 3.1   Days lost per thousand persons
employed in mining, manufacturing,
construction and transport 1951–62

Country	Days lost
USA	1,185
Italy	780
Canada	649
Japan	579
Belgium	501
Australia	462
France	391
UK	272
West Germany	77
Sweden	53

Source: Based on ILO statistics

fact, this period now appears as a unique interregnum in the twentieth century.

Socialism in the Fourth French Republic

In France and Italy 'tripartite' coalition governments of the three main political trends – Christian Democratic, Socialist and Communist – ruled their countries between 1945 and 1947. It was thought that the countries' problems were so great, following war losses, that only governments based on a broad consensus could solve them. The Communists and Socialists agreed on much in economic terms, favouring nationalisation and planning. The MRP in France, and the DC in Italy, championed private enterprise as much as they dared. All agreed on the need for welfare measures, with the Communists tending to outbid their rivals in their popular demands. In France, the welfare measures initiated by the prewar Popular Front government were built on, and a national planning mechanism was established which is thought to have played an important role in postwar French recovery. Until January 1946, when he resigned as head of the provisional government, De Gaulle dominated the political scene in France. He resigned because he could not persuade the Left to increase military expenditure. The coalition partners continued until May 1947 when their partners ejected the Communists from the government for their pro-Moscow position, promotion of industrial militancy and attempts to infiltrate their own supporters into the ministries which they controlled. France then faced a series of weak governments – there were twenty-one between 1944 and 1958. Of these ten were headed by the Radicals, four by the MRP and only two by the Socialists (SFIO).[14] The Socialists were under pressure from the Communists, the MRP and De Gaulle's supporters. Having found themselves attracting fewer votes in 1946 than the Communists, who emerged, with 28.6 per cent of the vote, as the largest party, they felt they could ill afford to appear to waver on their Marxist principles. Yet they were required to maintain the democratic Fourth Republic as they were the third largest party with 17.9 per cent of votes. The MRP, the second largest party, achieved a 26.4 per cent vote. Without SFIO support or tolerance in parliament it was difficult for governments to survive. Guy Mollet, Secretary General of the SFIO 1946–69, became an important facilitator or coalition bargainer[15] while only actually leading the government of 1956–7. This government proved to be the longest lasting of the Fourth Republic. Although Mollet took France into the disastrous Suez adventure (1956), on the positive side he helped to persuade the National Assembly, in January 1957, that France should agree to the terms negotiated for the setting up of the EEC.

Nevertheless, the SFIO found itself obliged to acquiesce in policies with which many of its voters disagreed.[16] Its support in the country dwindled from about 25 per cent in 1945 to roughly 15 per cent in 1951 and 17 per cent in January 1956. In the same two elections the Communists scored roughly 25.7 per cent.[17] SFIO voters were older than those of any other party except the Radicals and were more likely to live in the smaller towns. About one-third were manual workers, one-fifth were white-collar employees, and one-eighth were peasants.[18] Like Mollet himself, a considerable number of the declining party membership were teachers. In France, Italy, Germany and elsewhere Socialism was greatly hampered by the Cold War and by the fact that large numbers of admirable people lined up in the cul-de-sac of Stalinism. In this situation the Left could not reach its full potential. In France, as elsewhere in Europe, economic revival came more swiftly than early predictions had suggested, thus taking the edge off social discontent, which favours the Left. The Algerian war caused confusion on the Left and brought about a crisis that almost destroyed democracy.

On the night of 1 November 1954 Algerian nationalists (FLN) attacked French military and civilian targets. This signalled the start of the Algerian war of independence. The end of colonialism was accelerating across the globe. The Americans and the Soviets quickened the pace by wooing the colonial peoples as potential Cold War allies. The French had overrun Algeria in 1830. From 1881 northern Algeria formed an integral part of France. French settlers arrived, French cities were built. Algerians studied in France and a native Westernised elite was formed. But after 1945 the tide of Arab nationalism swept across the region. Neighbouring Morocco regained its independence from France and Spain in 1956. This made it easier for the Algerians to carry out their fight from the safe havens of Morocco and Tunisia. The Algerians had been influenced by the defeat of the French earlier in 1954 at Dien Bien Phu, where over 11,000 French troops surrendered to the North Vietnamese. This caused the French to withdraw from Vietnam. In face of the revolt the French used ever more brutal methods, which dented their image abroad. In opposition Guy Mollet had promised autonomy to Algeria, but in office he increased the military pressure on the rebels. The problem was that the million or so European settlers living there did not want to live in an independent Algeria, and France argued that native Algerians had the same rights as French settlers. The settlers, backed by elite units stationed in Algeria, rose against the government in May 1958, and the situation was only brought under control once De Gaulle was safely back in office a month later. The general demanded, and got, a presidential-style constitution, which became the Fifth Republic. This was backed by most of the democratic parties including the SFIO. Once it became clear that De Gaulle was seeking a settlement with the FLN other insurrections occurred, but these were put down, and in 1962 Algeria became independent. On the day De Gaulle came to power a section of the SFIO left the party and set up the Autonomous Socialist Party, later renamed the United Socialist Party. Although it only attracted 2 to 3 per cent of the popular vote it appeared a serious blow to the SFIO at the time.[19]

Spaak: Belgium's Socialists and the EEC

The Socialists in Belgium and Holland did not have to compete
with large Communist parties, but they had little chance of gaining
an absolute majority of votes. In both countries religious affiliation,
as well as class, was a key determinant of voting behaviour, and
Christian Democracy was strong. However, in Holland and Belgium
the Socialists gained in stature during the war and led governments
in the postwar period. The Dutch Socialists (PvdA) were in coalition
governments from the liberation to 1958. In the five elections
between 1946 and 1963 their average vote was 29 per cent. This
compared with an average for the three Christian parties of 50 per
cent all together. The Communist vote peaked at 10.6 per cent in
1946 and declined thereafter to 2.8 per cent in 1963. Willem Drees,
one of the first two Socialist ministers in 1939, led the PvdA in the
postwar period. He served as minister for social affairs between
1945 and 1948, during which time his old-age pensions legislation
brought him nationwide popularity. As prime minister, from 1948
to 1958, he saw Holland help to found NATO and the European
Coal and Steel Community (ECSC) which later broadened into the
EEC. His governments were responsible for the painful rehabilitation of a badly damaged economy with the help of Marshall Aid.
One important failure was decolonisation, although it could be
argued that the PvdA did not have charge of external and colonial
affairs. The Dutch attempted to hold on to their empire in the East
Indies (Indonesia) and, like the French, fought the local resistance
movements, which had been armed by the Americans in order to
fight the Japanese. By 1949 the Dutch had been persuaded to vacate
most of their overseas possessions, after the USA had concluded
that Communism was no longer a danger there.

In neighbouring Belgium the Socialist Party (PSB/BSP) headed
coalition governments from 1945 to 1949 and from 1954 to 1958.
It joined Christian Social Party-led governments from 1961 to 1966.
On average, in the five elections between 1946 and 1958 the Socialist
Party attracted 33.5 per cent of the vote. The Christian Social Party
gained 44.2 per cent. The Communist vote dropped from 12.6 per
cent in 1946 to 1.9 per cent in 1958. Socialist leader Paul Henri
Spaak had served as Belgium's first Socialist prime minister,
1938–9, and was foreign minister of the government-in-exile in
London during the war. He served as premier once again in 1946
and 1947–9. As foreign minister, 1954–7 and 1961–6, Spaak was a

pivotal figure in the founding of the EEC and NATO. His party had been in the reformist tradition since the First World War, when universal male suffrage was achieved. The other major Socialist leaders were Henry Van Acker and Camille Huysmans. Having emerged from the trade union movement, Van Acker became was prime minister from 1945 to 1946 and briefly again in 1946. The aged Huysmans headed the government 1946–7. The Socialists were opposed by the powerful Catholic Church, and the introduction of votes for women in 1949 helped to reinforce political Catholicism. The Socialists had originally looked for an ally in the Liberals, with whom they agreed on constitutional/libertarian issues. Indeed, the early postwar governments of Van Acker and Huysmans, August 1945 to March 1947, had included the Socialists, Liberals and Communists. The change came with the start of the Cold War, from which time the Communists, still the third largest party, were excluded from office. Under Spaak, the Socialists turned to the Christian Socials as a coalition partner. The two parties had more in common on social issues than they had with the Liberals. Among the key early postwar issues facing Spaak and his colleagues were what to do about the monarchy, and what to do about Belgium's relations with its neighbours. Leopold, King of the Belgians, was regarded by many at home and abroad as having been a collaborator during the Nazi occupation. He chose to remain in the country rather than leave with the government for Britain. His abrupt surrender to the Germans put his French and British allies in danger in 1940.

Belgium reached near civil war conditions in 1950 when Leopold attempted to take up his role as head of state once again. The Socialists and Communists, most of the Liberals and some Catholics wanted him to go, and the Catholic hierarchy wanted him to stay. The French-speaking elements in the country were mostly against him; most Flemings (Dutch-speakers) favoured him. A compromise was agreed and Leopold abdicated in favour of his son Baudouin. The Socialist movement worked to unite both French-speakers and Dutch-speakers. But differences were deep-rooted. The Dutch areas were more agricultural and more strongly Catholic; the French more industrialised and less Catholic. Cultural nationalism was a much stronger political force in Dutch-speaking Flanders than in French-speaking Wallonia. In 1954 the Volksunie broke into parliament with 2.2 per cent of the vote. The success of this Flemish nationalist party started the slide, which eventually led to all the parties and states becoming federal bodies based on language.

Given the conflicts over cultural identity – and having been overrun twice in twenty-six years – the Belgians were ready to seek solutions to their problems through membership of wider bodies. These they found in the OEEC, NATO and the ECSC, which later became the EEC. Spaak, as prime minister, played a major part in the Brussels Treaty of March 1948, which united Britain, France, Belgium, Holland and Luxembourg in a defensive alliance and was the forerunner of NATO. He chaired the committee which wrote the report that eventually led to the Treaty of Rome and the setting up of the EEC on 1 January 1958. The Socialists of Belgium, Holland and Luxembourg embraced the EEC and hoped to infiltrate their ideals into it. The French also accepted it with less enthusiasm in the early stages. The British and the Italian Left saw it as an American, German, capitalist and Vatican plot.

1948: Italy, 'Stalinism against God, Soviet Russia against America'

In a nutshell, it could be said that the Left was prevented from gaining power in Italy by Allied military occupation (to 1947), the influence of the Catholic Church, American material aid to Italy, Soviet and Yugoslav moves, Alcide De Gasperi's political cunning, and its own mistakes.

The occupation of Italy by American and British forces was a reminder that the Western powers were not indifferent to the fate of Italy. They did interfere in Italian affairs; and the military intervention by Britain in Greece had not been forgotten. In Italy the Church was enormously wealthy and could influence its flock through material as well as spiritual assistance. Italy was poor, unemployment was high, and the Church presided over a wide variety of institutions to help the poor, the old and the needy. Women, in particular, appreciated the rhetoric of the Christian Democrats (DC) about the importance of family values. Communism and Socialism were regularly denounced from the pulpit. The USA offered extensive economic aid to Italy even before Marshall Aid got under way. The Soviet Union could offer nothing. The Italians felt they knew the USA, as many of them had relatives or friends living there. It was much easier to trust the Americans than the little-known Soviet Union. In any case, the Soviet image had become increasingly tarnished due to the stories about

Soviet activities in Austria and reports from returning Italian prisoners of war. Such evidence rekindled old fears about Communism. In addition, Tito's Yugoslavia, with Soviet support, sought to annex the port of Trieste (Italian from 1918) and the surrounding area (in which large numbers of Slovenes were living). Following Moscow's line the PCI and PSIUP supported these moves. Most Italians rejected them. After much tension the peace treaty of 1947 internationalised the city and the surrounding area went to Yugoslavia. In 1954 Trieste was returned to Italy.

Stalin was not encouraging the PCI to take the insurrectionary road to Socialism. And Togliatti, the Communist leader, had no inclination to do so. The PCI's policy was one of broad alliances with the Socialists, the Christian Democrats, and all 'anti-Fascist progressive elements' in whichever class or party. The PCI was attempting to rival the Catholic Church, and its client, the DC, in building up a network of bodies to win support from all age groups, both sexes, and most social groups, not just the industrial workers. It was quite successful in doing this, offering its adherents a secular alternative to the social institutions of the Church and the DC.

Although in the first postwar Italian elections the Socialists (PSIUP) actually gained more votes than the PCI, they were never able in this period to establish their own political autonomy.[20] Headed by Pietro Nenni, they still saw the Soviet Union as the workers' state, and the PCI as its true ambassador in Italy. They were unable to formulate a reform strategy to suit Italian democratic politics. This was too much for Giuseppe Saragat, who led a breakaway, early in 1947, to form the Social Democratic Party of Italy (PSDI). With him went 52 of the PSIUP's 115 parliamentarians, but a much smaller percentage of the rank and file. The PSIUP was too small to exercise great influence with the DC and led something of a shadow existence.

The Church and the Americans gave all the help they could to the DC in the decisive election of 1948. From the USA, Cardinal Spellman declared:

> I cannot believe that the Italian people ... will choose Stalinism against God, Soviet Russia against America who has done so much and stands ready and willing to do so much more, if Italy remains a free, friendly and unfettered nation.[21]

The only 'help' Stalin provided was the Communist seizure of power in democratic Czechoslovakia at the end of February. A month later the DC swept back into office with an absolute majority of seats in parliament on 48.5 per cent of the vote. The PCI-PSIUP alliance gained 31 per cent. Saragat's Social Democratic PSDI attracted 7.1 per cent. In 1947 De Gasperi had followed the French example and dissolved his coalition with the PCI and the PSIUP. He now formed a coalition with the PSDI, the liberal Republicans, and the right-wing Liberals. He remained head of government until 1953; his party led governments without a break until the 1990s.

1957: Bonn, 'no experiments!'

By 1949 the Western powers felt enough progress had been made in West Germany to sanction the setting up of a new republic, the Federal Republic of Germany (FRG). A constitution was agreed at a constitutional convention and elections were held for the new parliament (Bundestag) in August 1949. The CDU and its Bavarian sister party, CSU, gained 139 seats to the SPD's 131. Voting was by a variant of the proportional representation (PR) system. The (Liberal) FDP won 52 seats, the KPD 17, the Bavarian Party 17, the (Conservative) German Party 17, the right-wing DRP 5, and other small groups 26. From West Berlin came five SPD, two CDU and one FDP member(s), but the Western powers stipulated that they should only have observer status, as the city remained under their ultimate military control. Adenauer outmanoeuvred Schumacher in building a right-of-centre coalition.

That the SPD had done worse than many expected was hardly surprising in retrospect. West Germany had come a long way by sticking to a path mapped out in agreement with the Allies. More than Schumacher, Adenauer appeared to be their man. Due to the war losses and the division of Germany, the structure of the electorate was to the advantage of the CDU/CSU. There were more women than ever before, and in Germany, as in many European countries, they tended to be more right of centre than their male compatriots. Many old SPD strongholds were in the Soviet Zone. West Germany also had a much higher percentage of Catholics than Germany as a whole, and their Church was opposed to the SPD. A relatively large number of West Germans lived in small towns or villages dependent on farming, and traditionally they were more right wing. Adenauer encouraged nominal Nazis to return to

public life; many did so. There was talk of a 'restoration'. Former
Nazis got their jobs back in the civil service, police, and judiciary, in
education and industrial management. They were grateful to
Adenauer. Finally, the SPD's policies were not entirely clear to
many of the electorate. Adenauer stood for close ties with the Allies
and a policy of integration with Germany's Western neighbours.
The SPD did not fundamentally object to this, but wanted to post-
pone such integration until further negotiations with the Soviet
Union had taken place over German reunification. The truth was
that the electorate did not think successful negotiations could be
concluded with Stalin. This view was strengthened by the Berlin
blockade and by the crushing of the rising in East Germany in June
1953 by Soviet armed forces (this incident is described in the next
chapter). Such events certainly helped Adenauer to improve his
position. Another factor was the wide international recognition the
FRG gained after 1949. The Soviets had set up the German
Democratic Republic (GDR) in their zone, but it remained isolated.
The death of Schumacher and his replacement by the loyal,
sensible, yet colourless Erich Ollenhauer[22] was also an advantage
for Adenauer. By the election of 1957, the disadvantage of the SPD
had grown. Abroad everyone was talking about West Germany's
'economic miracle'. The important Saar region had returned to
Germany after being under French control, the FRG had become
sovereign in 1955, and was a member of NATO. Moreover, in that
year Adenauer had gone to Moscow to negotiate with Stalin's heirs,
and had gained the release of thousands of Germans still held
captive. The FRG and the Soviet Union had recognised each other
diplomatically. Once again the Soviets came to Adenauer's aid. In
1956 they crushed the reform-Communist regime in Hungary,
killing thousands in the process. This undermined completely the
SPD's strategy of neutralism and quasi-pacifism. No wonder
Adenauer's CDU/CSU gained an absolute majority of votes, under
the campaign slogan 'no experiments!', the only time any party
succeeded in doing this up to 1998.

The SPD felt compelled to change its strategy and tactics. At Bad
Godesberg in 1959 it adopted a new programme. Adopted by 324
votes to 16, this programme was largely the work of Heinrich Deist,
Carlo Schmidt and Herbert Wehner. It all but threw out public
ownership. It also attempted to get across the idea that the SPD was
non-sectarian in its philosophical outlook. This was not new. At the
Hanover conference of the SPD in 1946 Schumacher had proclaimed

that it did not matter how a man came to Socialism – through Marx or the Sermon on the Mount – all were accorded equal rights in the party. The Frankfurt declaration of the Socialist International (1952) incorporated this idea, as did the preamble to the Berlin programme of the SPD in 1954.[23] Its opponents tried to cast doubt on such declarations.

'Legitimate and ... necessary function' of the private sector

The Korean War, 1950–3, in which US, British and other allied troops were fighting the Communist North Koreans, made life more difficult for Communists and pacifists everywhere. This war followed closely on the defeat of America's ally Chiang Kai-shek in China, where, in 1949, Communist armies triumphed under Mao Zedong. This event and the explosion by the Soviet Union in the same year of its first atomic bomb led to fears of Communist spies. In the USA, an anti-left, in many ways anti-Semitic, witch-hunt was inaugurated by Senator Joseph McCarthy. Under Stalin, a far worse witch-hunt was going on in Eastern Europe. Between 1949 and 1953, thousands of loyal Communists, including many leaders, were purged as 'Trotskyist-Titoists' or 'cosmopolitans' (Jews), and either executed or sent to labour camps.[24]

Having helped the image of Socialism during the war years, Stalin tarnished it in the postwar period. This damaged both the Communists in Europe and anyone else who preached Socialism. The Catholic Church used its great influence to convince people it was a mortal sin to vote for candidates supporting Socialism. People also turned away from the Left, influenced by a spate of books by Communist defectors. The US-backed Congress for Cultural Freedom united many of those who came to see Marxism and state Socialism as evil. George Orwell's *Nineteen Eighty-Four* influenced many who never read it. Nor should it be forgotten that the Socialist pacifist, and internationally acclaimed thinker Bertrand Russell argued that the West should use the nuclear bomb, if necessary, to stop Stalinist expansionism. Socialists looked for other ways to realise their ideals of equality and freedom.

In Britain some in the Labour Party thought the Soviet experience had weakened the appeal of state ownership. There was also the belief that equality could be achieved through redistributive taxation rather than further large-scale public ownership. This, it was believed, would also make Labour more electable by weakening business opposition to its policies. Those taking this view were grouped around the journal *Socialist Commentary*, edited by Rita Hinden. She argued, 'To eliminate all private capital is to open the road to totalitarianism.' She recognised that the private sector 'has a legitimate and indeed a necessary function to perform'.[25] Hugh Gaitskell, who led Labour from 1955 until his death in 1962, endorsed this view as did his supporters such as Tony Crosland, Douglas Jay and Roy Jenkins. He clashed with the Left when he attempted, unsuccessfully, to revise Clause 4 of the party constitution.

The explosion of prosperity in the 1950s also weakened those taking an apocalyptic view of the 'crisis of capitalism'. After the struggles of the interwar years and the horrors of the war, most electors wanted to relax and enjoy their modest prosperity. They were looking for a bit of fun, colour and glamour. In the USA the liberal Democrat Adlai Stevenson lost to conservative Republican Dwight D. Eisenhower in 1952. Massive borrowing to support foreign aid and armaments fuelled the American economy, as did cheap raw materials and the demand for private credit. In Britain in 1951 Labour gained more votes than any party had previously done, but still lost the election. The Conservatives then kept office until 1964. The West German Christian Democrats were in government until 1969. Against many expectations, Spanish dictator Franco clung on to power until his death in 1975. In France the Right ruled until 1981, and in Italy the DC led governments through to the 1990s. Only in the small Scandinavian states were the Social Democratic parties regarded as the natural parties of government. In Denmark the Social Democrats ruled either alone or in coalition from 1947 to 1950 and from 1953 to 1968. In Norway their term of office ran from 1945 to 1961, and in Sweden from 1945 to 1976. In all cases they concentrated on practical reform policies rather than Socialist ideological aims. Even in Norway where they enjoyed an absolute majority, nationalisation did not feature prominently. The Second World War and the Cold War forced the Scandinavian countries to re-evaluate their traditional policy of neutrality, and Norway and Denmark decided to join NATO. Partly for fear of provoking the Soviet Union, Sweden remained neutral. Finland had no option, being bound by its treaty with the Soviets. The Finnish Communist Party, legalised in 1944 and posing as part of a democratic alliance (SKDL), became a major force in politics and participated in government between 1944 and 1948. The Scandinavians, including Iceland, set up the Nordic Council, which resulted in a common labour market, abolition of passport controls and reciprocal social security arrangements.

Chapter 4

The Stalinist model in Eastern Europe
1945–61

1948: 'Trotsky's mantle falls on Tito's shoulders'

In theory, after 1945 the Communist parties were encouraged to support different national roads to Socialism which varied according to local conditions. In fact a pattern emerged across Soviet-occupied Europe. The governments or – in the ex-enemy states Germany, Bulgaria, Hungary and Romania – the Soviets got control of the commanding heights of the economy on the grounds that the former owners were Fascists or Nazi collaborators, or that such enterprises were 'enemy property'. This enabled the Soviet Union to exploit their economies more easily, and gave the local Communists greater power of patronage.[1] The Communists were 'advised' to join broad coalitions with other 'anti-Fascist' parties. This soon revealed itself to be the same strategy as that developed in the Spanish Republic – a smoke-screen behind which the Communists struggled for power with the help of Soviet forces. In Poland a virtual civil war was fought between Stalin's Polish Committee for National Liberation and the Home Army, the main resistance movement to the Nazis, supported by the government in exile in London. In 1945 the Smallholders Party won the elections in Hungary but they were forced into a renewed coalition with the Communists and Socialists. Another key step on the road to 'People's Democracy' was to force through mergers of the Communists with the Social Democrats to create a 'united working class party'. This happened in Poland, Hungary and the Soviet Zone of Germany. Pseudo 'bourgeois' or peasant parties were also established to weaken the authentic ones as in the cases of Bulgaria, Hungary, Poland and the Soviet Zone of Germany.[2] Everywhere trade union federations, youth movements, women's movements and leagues of culture were formed under Communist control. Increasingly, membership of appropriate bodies was essential to gain employment, education or advancement. But almost everywhere the Communists were easy prey for Stalin because they were 'Soviet patriots'. They could not conceive that the Soviet system was not only imperfect but also downright criminal. Their Marxism was in most cases too weak to withstand such a discovery. The exception was Tito and most of his comrades. Stalin fell out with Tito, who had appeared a most loyal follower. Tito, supported by most of his colleagues, dared to ignore Soviet advice on what was best for Yugoslavia's development.[3]

In 1948 the League of Yugoslav Communists was expelled from the Cominform. This body had been established in 1947 and all the ruling East European Communist parties (except that in Albania) belonged to it, as did the French and Italian parties. It subjected the Yugoslavs to a campaign of vilification. It was claimed that 'Trotsky's mantle falls on Tito's shoulders'.[4] Worse still, 'the Titoites' were 'part of a conscious, counter-revolutionary plan of direct agents of Anglo-American imperialism'.[5] Yugoslavia was faced with economic boycott by the Soviet bloc, military threats and attempts to foment revolt from within. There was also a plan to assassinate Tito.[6] However, the most serious international flashpoint was not Yugoslavia but Germany.

1948: German road 'serious theoretical blunder'

The Soviets had initially licensed four political parties – the KPD, the SPD, the CDU and the Liberals (LDPD) – in their zone of Germany. The four were forced to co-operate in the Anti-Fascist Front; competitive elections were not held. Fearing the SPD would emerge as the main party, the Soviets, in April 1946, had ensured the merger of the SPD with the KPD to form the Socialist Unity Party of Germany (SED). To win over the Social Democrats they had promised that the SED would be democratic and Marxist rather than Marxist-Leninist. Some Social Democrats genuinely believed this to be the way forward. They thought (wrongly) that the split in the working-class movement in 1933 had enabled Hitler to gain power. Some, not only Social Democrats, felt guilty about Nazi crimes in the Soviet Union, and were inclined, therefore, to accept Soviet wishes. Some were opportunists who just wanted to advance their careers by currying favour with the occupying power. Others were intimidated by the Soviet secret police. The Soviets reopened the Nazi concentration camps and filled them with anyone who opposed them. This included thousands of Social Democrats, Christian Democrats, Communists and, of course, Nazis.[7] Otto Grotewohl, a former member of the Reichstag, led the SPD into the SED with Wilhelm Pieck's KPD. In 1947, using intimidation and threats, the Soviet Military Administration got rid of Jakob Kaiser and Ernst Lemmer, the leaders of the CDU in the Soviet Zone. Both fled to the West, as did many of their party colleagues. On 24 September 1948 Anton Ackermann, writing in *Neues Deutschland*, recanted his thesis of a special 'German way' to Socialism. He now claimed that the contention that the German road to Socialism differed from the Soviet experience hindered the struggle for the SED to become a party of a new type, that is a party like the CPSU. For these reasons this 'serious theoretical blunder' had to be liquidated.[8] By the time the GDR was inaugurated in the autumn of 1949 it was, according to the theory, no different from the regimes in the other Soviet bloc states. In 1950 the setting up of the Ministry for State Security (MfS) further underlined this. It was to play a decisive role in the life of the GDR. On Soviet prompting in 1952 the SED agreed the 'planned building of the basis of Socialism in the GDR'. In the same year the existence of the armed forces of the GDR was made public. These 'police units' had started to form on military lines in 1948. Clearly, the GDR was well on the way to becoming a model Soviet-style state.

The GDR had the advantage of being a modern Western European society with possibly the most up-to-date economy in Europe. In the Soviet bloc only Czechoslovakia came close to being modern. In the Soviet Zone the most modern of German industries had been at home, including scientific precision instruments, office calculating equipment that represented the beginnings of the computer industry, electronics and much more. This territory also boasted a thriving agricultural sector. Its weakness was lack of raw materials, above all coal and steel. These had been brought from West Germany or Silesia, the latter now under Polish control. Another problem was the Soviet attempt to dismantle the factories and transfer them to the Soviet Union. Key personnel were rounded up and sent to work there. The constant loss of manpower to the

West also played havoc with plans for economic recovery. Thousands left every month, their numbers depending on the immediate political situation. Frequent changes of policy also slowed economic revival.[9]

On the whole, the other Soviet bloc states were well behind Western Europe in economic development. Much of the prewar Polish economy was devoted to subsistence farming. Postwar Poland took over German territories with industrial, mining and agricultural potential but was slow in mobilising that potential. Czechoslovakia expelled most of its skilled German population from the Sudeten area. It was not easily replaceable. Of the remaining areas, Bohemia had both modern and traditional industries. Slovakia was relatively backward. Bulgaria had good agriculture but little industry. Hungary was in a similar position. Apart from its oil industry Romania was poorly developed. Yugoslavia was largely underdeveloped both industrially and agriculturally. Its two western republics, Slovenia and Croatia, were closer to neighbouring Austria in their development. Albania was the poorest country in Europe. In addition, Poland and Yugoslavia in particular had suffered horrendous war losses. Rather than building on their existing industries the Communists followed the Soviet model of developing heavy industry, and neglecting light and consumer industries. In these circumstances poor living standards could only get worse.

All these states were beset by national, ethnic and religious antagonisms. They inherited disputed territories and harboured minorities with affiliations beyond their borders. Tito had sought to deal with this problem through a Balkan federation. Stalin vetoed this.

1952: Traitor Slansky 'in reality loyal Stalinist'

Communists everywhere sought to destroy all opposition, from whatever source, to their rule. Everywhere attempts were made to intimidate the Churches by trials and long prison sentences. In Hungary, for instance, the Catholic primate, Cardinal Mindszenty, was sentenced to life imprisonment in 1949. Political opponents, such as the former leaders of the Hungarian Socialist Party, were jailed. On top of this there were the purges which afflicted the ruling parties themselves. In the period prior to Stalin's death in

1953, the so-called 'Zionist-cosmopolitan-Trotsky-Tito' conspiracy consumed many leading Communists. It appears that Stalin wanted to use the Jewish community of the Soviet Union to secure financial help from Jewish organisations in the USA for the rehabilitation of the Soviet economy. To this end he supported the establishment of a Jewish state in Palestine. The aim was also to weaken British influence, then still strong, in the Middle East. After he failed to get such economic assistance he turned against the Jews. Once Israel was established in 1948 and looked to the USA rather than the Soviet Union for aid, Stalin saw the Jews as a national group with potentially divided loyalties.[10] Thousands of Jews lost their jobs, were arrested or worse. Soviet Foreign Minister Molotov was demoted in March 1949 and his Jewish wife was arrested. Abakumov, minister of state security from 1946, was arrested in July 1951, because, for Stalin, he 'knew too much'.[11]

In the satellite states many of the leading figures were removed, forced to confess their 'crimes' at show trials and then executed. This was the fate of Kochi Xoxe in Albania, Traicho Kostov in Bulgaria, Laszlo Rajk in Hungary, Anna Paulka in Romania, all in 1949. In 1952 it was the turn of Rudolf Slansky, General Secretary of the Czechoslovak Communist Party, 'in reality a loyal Stalinist'.[12] In all cases they were tried with others. That these Communists confessed to being traitors and Western intelligence agents can be explained by torture, threats to their families, a sense of duty to the party, and promises of freedom under false names.[13]

1953: 'Eternal glory to the memory of Joseph Stalin'

The nineteenth Congress of the CPSU assembled in Moscow on 5 October 1952. It was the first Congress for over thirteen years, and the last that Stalin would attend. Now aged nearly 73, he hardly spoke, but his presence dominated the scene. Before the Congress his *Economic Problems of Socialism in the USSR* had been published. This was a rambling collection of his thoughts covering domestic and foreign policies. The prediction that most caught the world's attention was his view that war between the capitalist states was more likely than war between the Soviet Union and the West.[14] Stalin's silence was adequately compensated for by the speech of his mouthpiece Malenkov, and to a lesser degree by Khrushchev. By the end of the Congress Malenkov appeared to be the natural successor to Stalin.

The death of Stalin on 5 March 1953 hit the world Communist movement hard. Communists everywhere experienced gloom, fear and even despair. The British Communist leader Harry Pollitt wrote in the *Daily Worker*:

> Never the dictator, never one to lay down the law, always eager and willing to listen, to understand another's point of view. ... No words, no monuments, no tributes can ever do justice ... to the work of Comrade Stalin. ... Eternal glory to the memory of Joseph Stalin.

At the time of Stalin's death the surviving leaders had agreed among themselves to take measures to avoid disorder and panic. Both party and government leadership were streamlined. The government was headed by a five-man Presidium led by Malenkov. The party Presidium was reduced in size, including Malenkov and Beria and eight others.[15] Malenkov appeared to be becoming the new Stalin, but on 14 March he was forced to relinquish his position as party secretary. Khrushchev took on this post.

Beria appeared briefly to be in the ascendancy. He had served as minister of internal affairs between 1938 and 1945, when he was put in charge of overseeing the development of the Soviet Union's nuclear weapons project. A member of the party Presidium and a deputy head of government, he took over an even bigger Ministry of State Security. He began releasing prisoners, seeking better relations with Yugoslavia and putting out feelers about German reunification. He was arrested on 26 June. The remaining leaders continued most of the policies of Beria, who was shot on spurious treason charges in December.

1953: Berlin, 'We really did not know the mood ... of the people'

On 9 June 1953 the ruling Politburo of the SED announced a 'New Course'. This followed a similar development in the Soviet Union. It meant more emphasis on the production of consumer goods, the abolition of recent price rises and the cancelling of recent impositions on the remaining private businesses, peasants and intelligentsia. For instance, the children of small shopkeepers were unlikely to be allowed to study. The introduction of higher productivity norms (without pay increases) on the industrial workers was not rescinded.

The result was the outbreak of strikes starting with the prestige project, Stalinallee, in East Berlin, where construction workers downed tools and marched in protest. Strikes then spread to 271 other cities and towns in the GDR. Although only 5.5 per cent of the total workforce were said to have joined in, this represented a severe blow to the SED. Like the Stalinallee strikers, most of the others were workers at key or prestige factories or sectors of the economy. Moreover, it was inconceivable for the Communist leaders that workers would strike against 'their party' and 'their government'. As Markus Wolf, head of the East German intelligence service, was to write in his memoirs, 'We really did not know the mood of wide sections of the people.'[16] The East German regime was only prevented from collapse by the protection afforded it by the Soviet army and the imposition of martial law.

Ulbricht had been on the verge of being removed as leader of the SED. The revolt saved him, as the Soviet leadership felt that they had to support a compliant client. The malaise in the GDR political system was revealed in the membership of its parliament, the Volkskammer. Of the 400 members 'elected' in 1950, eight had been arrested by the MfS, seventeen had fled to the West, and forty-four had been forced by the SED to resign. Only 180 were 're-elected' in 1954.[17]

1956: Khrushchev on Stalin's 'cult of the individual'

By 1955 Khrushchev had defeated his rival Malenkov by getting his temporary ally Bulganin installed as head of government in place of Malenkov. Khrushchev and Bulganin then toured the world in an attempt to repair the damage done by Stalin's policies. They improved relations with Finland and Iran, visited Britain, made a successful tour of India and ate humble pie in Yugoslavia. Austria was freed from four-power occupation in 1955 and the Soviet Union established relations with West Germany. The image of the Soviet Union rose correspondingly. At home Khrushchev started quietly rehabilitating some of Stalin's victims and degrading the dead leader. However, no one expected Khrushchev's 'secret' speech at the twentieth Congress of the CPSU in February 1956. He accused Stalin of having left the Leninist path, having pursued the 'cult of the individual', and of incompetence and murder. He told the delegates that of the 139 members and candidates of the party's Central

Committee who were elected at the seventeenth Congress in 1934, ninety-eight persons, that is 70 per cent, were arrested and shot (mostly in 1937–8). A majority of the delegates to the 1934 Congress met the same fate. Stalin, he said, had had thousands of Soviet officers killed in the 1930s, had ignored numerous warnings about the Nazi onslaught in 1941 and had made colossal military blunders. He had deported 'whole nations', accusing them of being disloyal. After the war he continued to pursue the 'cult of the individual', used terror methods against his colleagues, caused the rupture of relations with Yugoslavia, retarded Soviet agriculture and fabricated the 'doctors' plot'.

Khrushchev gave his speech in closed session, claiming that he did not want to give ammunition to the enemies of the Soviet Union. Clearly the Soviet leaders realised that it was in all their interests to 'liquidate' the Stalin cult, end his methods of leadership change, and attempt to organise their state on a more rational basis. They had to be careful not to bring down the whole system by their attacks on Stalin's methods, and they were conscious that they could be accused of having supported Stalin throughout their own rise to eminence. For these reasons, although Khrushchev's speech was devastating for those who had believed in Stalin, its scope was also limited. Stalin's work against the Trotskyists and others in the 1920s and 1930s was regarded as sound. Nor were the horrors of land collectivisation acknowledged. Khrushchev fell back on the works of Lenin and the cult of his personality for future guidance, even though Lenin had helped, both in theory and practice, to establish the system that gave rise to Stalin and Stalinism.

The 'secret speech' reached the West via a Soviet defector and was made available by the US Information Service.[18] It was one of the greatest news coups of the twentieth century. Summaries of it were discussed in other East European Communist parties.[19] It was not reported in the media of the Soviet Empire but portraits of Stalin disappeared from offices and other public places, towns and villages named after him were renamed, statues of him disappeared, sometimes at dead of night (e.g. in East Berlin), and his works were withdrawn and placed in 'the dustbin of history'. A limited 'thaw' brought liberation for thousands of prisoners and greater freedom in the arts. Solzhenitsyn had his sentence for 'anti-Soviet agitation' annulled in April 1956.[20] His book, about the labour camps, *One Day in the Life of Ivan Denisovich*, was published in 1962 with the approval of Khrushchev.[21]

Tito's 'New Class'

Tito had cut a heroic figure in Britain during the war as the tough patriotic Yugoslav whose activities were holding down masses of German troops. Most people were unaware of the national and political rivalries within Yugoslavia. At the end of the war there was disappointment when Tito appeared to be Stalin's man. After 1948 Tito was presented as an increasingly attractive figure by the media in the West. British, French and US aid was granted to Yugoslavia. Tito was forced to reassess his situation both internally and externally. In external affairs he skilfully carved out a place for himself as one of the key members of the non-aligned states. Other leaders included Nehru of India, Nasser of Egypt and Sukarno of Indonesia. At home he had to make his regime appear different from the Soviet bloc, which was detested by most Yugoslavs – especially outside Serbia – yet satisfy his party comrades that he was not turning his back on Marxism-Leninism. He sought to do this by unravelling the collective farm system, giving more autonomy to the individual republics, and introducing a system of Workers' Self-Management in 1950. The name of the party was changed to League of Communists of Yugoslavia. It is difficult to be certain how much more than cosmetic these changes were. His close friend and aide, Vice-Premier Milovan Djilas, who helped to rethink Socialism in Yugoslavia, concluded the system was incompatible with freedom. In his book *The New Class*, published in the USA, he claimed that the new rulers of Yugoslavia, like their Soviet counterparts, were worse than the capitalists had been. Although he was imprisoned he was better treated than others like him in the Soviet bloc. He outlived the system.

1956: The tragedy of Hungary

The other states within the Soviet orbit followed Khrushchev's line on Stalin. Everywhere his victims were quietly rehabilitated. One of them was Wladyslaw Gomulka in Poland. On 21 October 1956 he was elected First Secretary of the ruling United Workers' Party. His election successfully defused a desperate situation. Earlier in the year there had been widespread strikes and clashes between strikers and police. Poland appeared on the verge of revolution. Gomulka offered hope of better times. He ensured greater intellectual freedom, reversed the collectivisation of agriculture, temporarily eased the burdens of the workers and sought dialogue with the powerful Catholic Church. Cardinal Wyszynski backed Gomulka, as did, from afar, the Chinese. Meanwhile the Soviet leaders were embroiled in a much worse situation in neighbouring Hungary.

It was difficult to believe that the Soviet leaders who had denounced Stalin would send their tanks into a country allied to them. But this is what they did on 4 November 1956.[22] The tanks were met with resistance, and great loss of life occurred. In the end, Hungary could not stand against the might of the Soviet juggernaut. The crisis began after the Hungarian Communists rehabilitated some of Stalin's victims, including Rajk. In July, Stalinist Rakosi was sacked on Soviet orders and was replaced by Erno Gerö as party leader. Rapprochement with Tito followed. Expectations grew over the summer, and in October anti-Stalinist demonstrations occurred in Budapest. To placate the masses Imre Nagy, a former prime minister identified with the reform course, was asked to head a new government. Nagy attempted to keep up with the demands from below and formed a genuine coalition government. In an effort to appease his new colleagues Nagy, thought by some to be a KGB agent,[23] made the fatal mistake of promising that he would take Hungary out of the Warsaw Pact. The invasion followed and Janos Kadar was installed as Moscow's man. Nagy paid with his life.

1959: Khrushchev, 'We will bury you'

Having avoided the disintegration of the Soviet Empire in Eastern Europe, Khrushchev turned his attention to economic affairs. Part of de-Stalinisation was to put the economy on a sounder footing. In any case, more genuine dialogue with the masses had exposed the great dissatisfaction with prevailing living standards. He dealt with this at the twenty-first Congress of the CPSU in 1958. He promised his audience that the Soviet Union would overtake the USA in per capita consumption levels of basic goods by 1970.[24] On 10 July 1958, at the fifth Congress of the SED, Ulbricht made a similar, and equally unrealistic promise – that the GDR would overtake West Germany by 1961.[25] He reminded the delegates and representatives of forty-six other parties that their Chinese comrades had pledged to overtake Britain in crucial industrial sectors in less than fifteen years.[26] How differently it was all to turn out!

Why was Ulbricht so optimistic? He was of course following his

Soviet master, who was at the SED congress. The optimism was in part due to the renewal process after the death of Stalin. Far more, it owed much to Soviet achievements in space, aviation and education. The Soviet Union had surprised the world with the speed with which it had mastered nuclear technology, exploding its first atomic bomb in 1949 and a hydrogen bomb in 1953, only months after the first comparable US bomb. More recently, it had astonished the world by being the first state to place an artificial satellite in space (4 October 1957). In 1959 the unmanned Soviet rocket, Lunik II, became the first human-made object to reach the moon's surface. The Soviet Union put the first man, Yuri Gagarin, into space in 1961 and the first woman, Valentina Tereshkova, in 1963. Soviet scientists won the Nobel prize for physics in 1958 and 1962, and were joint winners in 1964. Western observers rightly emphasised that, despite help from spies like Klaus Fuchs,[27] the Soviets could only achieve these results because they had a well-organised army of scientists and technologists. These coups led Western experts to give credence to other Soviet claims of achievements in welfare, education and the economy, but these were far from real. They also misled the Soviet leaders themselves into setting unrealistic targets. In the 1970s villages near Moscow still had no running water, and Moscow and Leningrad shops were a sorry sight indeed.[28] One British ICL manager, sent in 1969 to organise courses for Soviet computer specialists, was surprised by the poor organisation and primitive equipment available. Muscovites lived with 'frustrating bureaucracy and unending dreariness'.[29] Yet, in buoyant mood, Khrushchev warned the West, 'We will bury you.'[30]

One other cause for optimism in the Communist movement was the rapid decolonisation of Western empires. In April 1956 twenty-nine states, mainly Afro-Asian, met in Bandung to form the Non-Aligned Movement. The French had been forced to quit Indo-China (Vietnam) in 1956. Ghana had gained its independence from Britain in 1957, proclaiming African Socialism. Britain had been forced to call off its invasion of Egypt in 1957 and faced an emergency in Cyprus. The French were on their way out of Algeria. Iraq was proclaimed a republic in 1958 after the assassination of the Western ally King Faisal. In the same year British troops were sent to Jordan and US marines landed in Lebanon. Western imperialism appeared to be rapidly disintegrating.

1961: Berlin, 'I know the Wall is an ugly thing'

By the time the GDR was supposed to be overtaking West Germany it appeared to be once again on the verge of collapse. After dropping to 'only' 204,092 in 1958 and 143,917 in 1959, the numbers of East Germans fleeing the GDR rose again in 1960 to 199,188.[31] The bulk of them left the GDR via Berlin, which, although divided into four sectors – Soviet, British, French and US – was not yet physically divided. The main East German border with West Germany had been impassable since 1952. The most important reason for this flight was the declining economic situation. As more left the situation for those left behind got worse. The economy had been thrown off course by changes demanded by the GDR's biggest customer, the Soviet Union, by the collectivisation of agriculture 1959–60, and by higher defence spending. Young men were fleeing because they were pressured to 'volunteer' for military service. In 1961 a kind of panic developed. The threats made by Khrushchev to the position of the Western allies in Berlin had caused Berliners to fear that another 1948-style crisis, or worse, was brewing. The failure of talks between Khrushchev and US President J.F. Kennedy in June increased fears.[32] In July alone 30,000 turned their backs on the GDR.[33] Something would have to be done to stop the haemorrhage. In the early hours of 13 August 1961 something *was* done. With the approval of Moscow, armed East German troops and police started to seal off East Berlin from the three Western sectors of the city. They stopped the metropolitan railway, turned back motor traffic in both directions, barricaded streets leading to the West and started erecting what was to become the notorious Berlin Wall. Willy Brandt later pointed out that Kennedy had said to Khrushchev in Vienna that what happened in the GDR was up to Khrushchev. The USA could not and would not get involved in decisions taken by the Soviets in their own sphere of influence.[34] He seemed to be giving the Soviets the green light to restore order in the GDR. At any rate, the Western powers felt they could do little other than verbally condemn Soviet actions. The Wall gave the GDR leaders a breathing space, but it represented a permanent anti-Communist propaganda monument seen every year by hundreds of thousands of tourists. Even Khrushchev is reported to have said, 'I know the Wall is an ugly thing. And it will come down some day'.[35]

Chapter 5

Democratic Socialists, Communists and the New Left

1956–68

1956: Togliatti, 'we cannot speak of a single guide'

The Western Communist parties were hit hard by Khrushchev's revelations about Stalin and by the suppression of the Hungarian revolution. The Italian party lost 250,000 members at this time.[1] In the 1950s New Left groups emerged throughout Western Europe. This was especially so in the Nordic countries. In Denmark Aksel Larsen broke with the Communists and set up the Socialist People's Party (SF). In Norway elements of the left wing of the Social Democrats and disaffected Communists established the Socialist People's Party (SF).[2] In Sweden a split was avoided because the Swedish Communists took up a more independent position vis-à-vis Moscow. In Finland, armed with a new programme stressing the democratic road to Socialism, the Communist-led alliance SKP/SKDL gained its best result in the elections of 1958.[3] In the coming years there was to be a plethora of left-wing parties in the Scandinavian states.

In France, after the invasion of Hungary, the PCF did lose the friendship of highly respected intellectuals Jean-Paul Sartre and Simone de Beauvoir and popular actors Yves Montand and Simone Signoret. However, it survived the revelations about Stalin and the invasion of Hungary largely unscathed. Public opinion polls revealed that only 5 per cent of PCF voters felt any indignation at the Hungarian repression.[4] As we saw in Chapter 3, a New Left type party, the Autonomous Socialist Party, was formed in 1958. Set up by André Philip after his expulsion from the SFIO, it advocated industrial democracy and self-management.[5] By becoming associated with former Premier Pierre Mendès-France the party attracted more publicity than its vote justified.

The Italian Communists were far more troubled by Khrushchev's denunciation of Stalin and by the Soviet invasion of Hungary. Palmiro Togliatti, Italian Communist leader, criticised the CPSU for not offering a Marxist analysis of Stalinism and argued that in the Communist movement 'we cannot speak of a single guide'.[6] His argument was that the development of Socialism and left-wing movements had become so complex that reality could not just be seen from one centre, that is Moscow. At the same time the Italian Socialist (PSI) leader Pietro Nenni decided it was time for his party to proclaim its independence from the Communists. Nenni started discussions with Saragat about possible reunification of the Social Democrats with the PSI. Only in 1959 did Nenni convince the majority of his colleagues that this was the right move. Four years later the PSI came in from the cold and entered a coalition government.[7]

1957: New Left 'jumble-sale of theoretical elements'

Communist Party of Great Britain (CPGB) membership slumped from 33,095 in 1956 to 26,742 in 1957 and 24,900 in 1958.[8] It is difficult today to understand what it meant to be a member of the CPGB and what it meant to leave it. Members were often scorned and ridiculed by outsiders and sometimes victimised by employers. The security service kept an eye on them. The CPGB 'was thoroughly penetrated at almost every level by technical surveillance or informants'.[9] Members often had very close personal relations with each other rather than with non-members. As an embattled minority, they clung together.[10] This made it more difficult to give up membership. 'Renegades' suffered terrible problems of conscience. The Communist parties were also extremely difficult to reform. They were structured to give all the advantages to the full-time party officials, the 'professional revolutionaries'.[11] As there was a high turnover of membership most ordinary members, with little experience, could easily be out-debated by the leaders. They could easily be expelled too. Most former Communists joined the Labour Party. Some did so because they were interested in careers in the unions or in parliament. Many more did so because they wanted to feel they were still carrying on the 'working class struggle'. They had given up their party but not their ideals. As there was a large exodus from the CPGB in this period, former members could stay in touch both personally and politically and attempt something new.

Former Communists played a major part in creating the 'New Left', a loose movement formed around the journals *New Reasoner* and *Universities and Left Review*. These eventually merged to become the *Left Review*. Among the leading 'New Leftists' were ex-Communists John Saville and Edward Thompson, lecturers at Hull and Leeds universities respectively, and the student activist Raphael Samuel. A key figure among the non-Communists was the West Indian and later professor of sociology at the Open University, Stuart Hall. The movement put on highly successful meetings with speakers including such ex-Communists as Clive Jenkins, the white-collar trade union leader, John Horner of the Fire Brigades Union, Doris Lessing, the writer, Ralph Miliband, the LSE academic, and Raymond Williams. In Scotland, Lawrence Daly left the CPGB and set up the Fife Socialist League (FSL), which defeated Communist councillors in local elections in one of their few strongholds as well as Communists in the National Union of Mineworkers (NUM).[12] Daly eventually became national secretary of the NUM. The New Left opened café bars in several towns including London and Manchester.

What was the significance of the New Left in Britain? Raymond Williams called it 'that jumble-sale of theoretical elements' brought together by 'a common sense of political crisis'.[13] It was not Trotskyist, rather Left libertarian, at a time when Britain was still a smug, class-ridden, imperialist society. It helped thousands to remain in politics who would otherwise have given up their interest. It provided a ginger group to touch the consciences of the Labour leaders. It attracted young people who felt little sympathy for either the Communist or the Labour parties. Although too much should not be made of the New Left, it seems likely that if Britain had had a system of proportional representation, a New Left party could have gained entry into parliament. As it was, Britain's electoral system reduced the options. Only by making the Labour Party Socialist, could British capitalism be defeated.

1957: Bevan, 'naked into the conference chamber'

Others turned to the New Left in Britain because they hated British establishment smugness and were alarmed by the Conservative government's foreign and defence policies. In particular, there was the Anglo-French-Israeli attack on Egypt at the very time the Soviets were pounding Budapest. Briefly, this was the Anglo-French response to Egyptian President Nasser's nationalisation of the Suez Canal and his general policy of asserting his country's independence from its previous 'protectors', Britain and France. The invasion was called off after it failed to get US backing and sterling went into free fall, badly damaging the economy.

The founding of the Campaign for Nuclear Disarmament (CND) in 1958, after an appeal in the *New Statesman* by the writer J.B. Priestley, both aided and weakened the New Left. Like the New Left, CND was a loosely organised movement of individuals in the arts, middle-class radicals and pacifist-inclined Labour MPs such as Frank Allaun and Michael Foot. CND focused entirely on the nuclear threat rather than the working-class struggle. Although predominantly left wing, it emphasised that it was open to all, irrespective of party or faith. In that it was critical of all the nuclear powers, it was *de facto* New Left on this issue. Both Labour and the CPGB had difficulties with CND's policy of unilateral nuclear disarmament for Britain. The CPGB, which had its own peace movement – the British Peace Committee – supported the Soviet line on a negotiated reduction of nuclear weapons. As the CPGB realised it had seriously underestimated CND's ability to mobilise young people it changed its stance in 1960, urging its members to take part in CND marches and demonstrations.[14] The *Daily Worker* was the only daily paper to back CND. The membership of the CPGB started to show a modest net increase in the early 1960s.[15]

Labour too agonised over CND. The leader of its left wing, Nye Bevan, at first supported unilateral nuclear disarmament, but changed his position on becoming deputy leader of the party. In 1957, opposing a unilateralist resolution, he claimed it would, if passed, send a foreign minister 'naked into the conference chamber'. The bomb would give Britain a 'modifying, moderating and mitigating influence'.[16] With the help of the block votes of the big trade unions the resolution was defeated at the annual party conference. The unilateralists won a temporary victory in 1960, only to have it reversed in 1961. By that time Bevan had died of cancer. His more right-wing colleague, Labour leader Hugh Gaitskell, died suddenly in 1963, some say as a result of a Soviet assassination plot.[17] Both men were only 63. Harold Wilson, who succeeded Gaitskell, had made his way by wooing the Left, by his television skills, and his reputation as an economist. His election caused some consternation in Washington. Paradoxically, Wilson's election as Labour leader greatly weakened the New Left and CND – many felt they did not want to 'rock the boat' and spoil Labour's chance of an election victory. Within the Labour Party itself, various groups, such as Victory For Socialism, in some ways close to the New Left and CND, suspended their activities. In 1964 Labour won the election with a majority of only four seats after thirteen years in the wilderness.

1958: Mao, 'paper tigers'

Despite being demonised in the US media, Mao Zedong's Communists received a fairly sympathetic welcome in Europe after they won the civil war and set up the People's Republic of China in 1949. In liberal and left-wing circles China was widely seen as a long-term underdog, a nation humiliated by the imperialist powers, especially Britain and Japan. After the overthrow of the Empire in 1911 by Sun Yatsen, numerous attempts were made to modernise the state and society, yet China sank still deeper into chaos, division and poverty. Chiang Kai-shek failed to expel the invading Japanese or unite the country. The Americans backed him as a bulwark against Mao's Communists after 1945, but he lost to them as head of what most observers regarded as a corrupt, inefficient and ruthless regime. He fled with the remnants of his followers to Taiwan where he presided over an economic miracle. Largely as a result of Western authors such as Edgar Snow,[18] Mao's image was that of a simple-living intellectual who commanded an army of loyal soldiers drawn largely from the downtrodden peasantry. Mao's massacres on the road to power, and afterwards, received little attention. Partially isolated by the Americans, Mao turned to Moscow for practical assistance and ideas. He and his colleagues such as Zhou Enlai believed the Soviet Union to be a successful Socialist experiment. This was 'proved' by its defeat of Nazi Germany and mastery of nuclear power.[19] Soviet advisers went to China and it adapted to the Soviet model.

The Chinese backed Khrushchev on Stalin, but did not entirely dismiss Stalin, backed the Yugoslavs but also criticised them, and supported Soviet actions in Hungary. However, by the 1960s Moscow and Beijing were openly at loggerheads. Old resentments dated back to the interwar period when the Chinese had built up their forces among the peasantry rather than relying on the workers in China's few industrial centres. Beijing regarded the visit of Khrushchev to the USA in 1959 as pandering to imperialism. The Americans had still not recognised Communist China. The Chinese alleged US and Indian involvement in the Tibet revolt against Communist rule in 1959. Although they compromised at the Moscow meeting of eighty-one Communist parties in 1960, the Soviets withdrew their advisers from China in the same year, causing great harm to the Chinese economy. By December 1962 they were in open dispute after years of the Soviets attacking the Albanians (allies of China), and the Chinese attacking the Yugoslavs (as proxies for Moscow). The Chinese had border disputes with India and the Soviet Union. Fighting broke out between China and India in 1962. This disturbed the Soviets who enjoyed excellent relations with India and provided it with military and economic aid. Later the Soviets and China clashed on their long frontier. Mao was often accused by Western Communists of ignoring the threat of nuclear war. His pronouncement that 'Imperialism and reactionaries are paper tigers' was often quoted as evidence of this. Mao had first used this turn of phrase in 1946 and repeated it in 1958. He was emphasising that an enemy can be a real tiger at one point but due to armed struggle becomes a paper tiger. He gave the Tsar of Russia and Hitler as examples.[20] This did not mean that the Communists were indifferent to nuclear war. However, the Central Committee of the Communist Party of China claimed: 'The emergence of nuclear weapons can neither arrest the progress of human history nor save the imperialist system from its doom.'[21]

1959: Castro, 'No dictatorship by one man'

The world held its breath between 16 and 28 October 1962. It appeared to be on the brink of a nuclear war. The crisis spot was the Caribbean island of Cuba. A former Spanish colony, Cuba had been run by a succession of US-backed dictators. US companies controlled the economy, and American gangsters controlled the leisure industry in the capital, Havana. Fidel Castro sought to change this when his guerrillas seized control of the country in 1959. In October 1960 President Eisenhower imposed a trade embargo on Cuba. The new US President, J.F. Kennedy, agreed on an invasion by CIA-trained exiles, which had been initiated by his predecessor. This was launched in April 1961 but failed immediately. Cuba was forced more and more into dependence on the Soviet Union. In 1962 Khrushchev gave military aid and installed missiles on the island. As the missiles could hit the USA, Kennedy could not ignore them. The crisis was averted when Khrushchev agreed to withdraw the missiles in exchange for US assurances that Cuba would not be invaded. Cuba lost much of its original appeal to the Left as it modelled its economic and political systems on those of the Soviet bloc.

Castro, a lawyer, had tried parliamentary politics before turning to the gun.[22] He was not a Communist, though his brother Raul was. Indeed, his guerrilla movement had been denounced by the urban-based Cuban Communists. In 1959, visiting the USA, he had claimed his was a humanist revolution: 'Humanism means social justice with liberty and human rights. ... No bread without liberty, no liberty without bread; no dictatorship by one man, no dictatorship by classes, groups, castes.'[23] The day after the Bay of Pigs invasion he declared that the revolution was Socialist. In July 1961 he integrated all the left-wing forces, including the Communists (PSP), into one body. This was transformed into the Cuban Communist Party (PCC) in 1965. Castro needed the Communists because they provided the administrators and urban-orientated cadres necessary to run the state. Castro's handsome Argentinian deputy Che Guevara, who had given up the medical profession to become a professional revolutionary, left Cuba in 1967 to foment revolution in Bolivia. There on 9 October 1967 he became a martyr and a revolutionary icon in both America and Europe.

The US attempts to overthrow Castro were just part of Washington's determination to maintain control of its unofficial empire. It overthrew, either directly or indirectly, the governments of British Guiana (1953), Guatemala (1954), the Dominican Republic (1965) and Chile (1973), and controlled Costa Rica, El Salvador, Honduras, Panama and other states in the region. These activities influenced the Left's attitude to the USA.

1966: China, 'repudiate ... reactionary bourgeois academic "authorities" '

On 18 August 1966 thousands of young Chinese 'Red Guards' appeared in Beijing's Tiananmen Square to celebrate the 'Great Proletarian Cultural Revolution'. Superficially the phraseology sounded fine. They were going to break with Soviet-style bureaucracy, with hierarchy, they were going to 'repudiate ... reactionary bourgeois academic "authorities"' who put a brake on the creativity of the masses. They were going to crush the 'capitalist roaders' and they were going to 'put daring above everything else'.[24] Either out of genuine fear that the revolution was becoming conservative or because he feared he would be overthrown by his comrades in the leadership of the Communist Party, Mao called this movement into life, but by autumn 1966 he was alarmed by the chaos he had unleashed. China was in danger of descending into warring factions as thousands died at the hands of the Red Guards or were driven to suicide. Mao started to denounce the Red Guards as politically immature and by summer 1968 he called in the People's Liberation Army to restore order. Gradually more moderate forces under Zhou Enlai gained the upper hand in the party. Both Zhou and Mao died in 1976. Within weeks of Mao's death the party moved to oust his widow and her radical clique, the 'Gang of Four'. Renounced in China, the ideas of the Cultural Revolution found favour among radicals beyond its borders. The *Little Red Book* of the thoughts of Chairman Mao looked like becoming an ersatz Bible.

1968: 'Fuck you, America!'

It has been written[25] that the message of Dennis Hopper's film *Easy Rider*, about disaffected drug-pushing American youth, was 'Fuck you, America!' The year was 1968 and in many countries, including the USA, students seemed to be saying just that. American culture – clothes, pop music, slang – had 'invaded' Europe. The USA was loved and hated at the same time. The impact of Hollywood films, usually more lavish and faster-moving than European films hampered by low budgets and language barriers, was immense. Many American movies frightened their audiences about the state of America. There were films such as *Rebel Without A Cause* (1955) with cult figure James Dean, anti-militarist films such as *Paths of Glory* (1957), and terrifying films about the coming nuclear holocaust such as *On The Beach* (1959) and *Dr Strangelove* (1964). In *Seven Days In May* (1964) the USA was on the verge of being taken over by the military-industrial complex (had not President Eisenhower himself warned about this?). Meanwhile the 'silent majority' was 'lost in a ceaseless ritual of martinis and barbecues' – *The Graduate* (1964).[26] These critical Hollywood films were augmented by similar efforts in Europe. The students of 1968 had grown up under such influences.

Another great influence came from the academic critics of capitalism who were not members of Communist or Trotskyist organisations. C. Wright Mills, professor of sociology at Columbia University, dissected America's new *Power Elite* (1959), Kenneth Galbraith wrote about 'private affluence and public squalor', and Herbert Marcuse about 'repressive tolerance'. At a practical level there was the struggle for civil rights by black people and, after 1964, the increasing ferocity of the Vietnam War. Although a majority of Americans supported President Johnson's attempts to stem the Communist advance in Vietnam in 1964, by 1968 they no longer believed victory was possible. By then Johnson had raised US troop levels to 685,000. In that year Richard Nixon was elected president by promising he would end the war. Vietnam was the world's first television war and Americans saw it nightly on their screens. Their 19-year-old sons were being conscripted to fight there. Many became casualties. The war cost the US 56,226 dead and 303,601 wounded.[27] In August 1972 the last US ground troops were pulled out. It was easy to interpret the war as a battle between a big rich bully and a poor little guy fighting to be free. Many people around the world saw it in these terms. Both the war and the opposition to it at American universities were seen on television in many countries. It provoked furious opposition among students in Europe and Australia. America claimed to be fighting for freedom in Vietnam, yet black people did not have the same degree of freedom in the USA as white people. Martin Luther King, the black preacher from Georgia, personified their struggle. King was assassinated in 1968. In the 1950s television showed police clubbing peaceful black demonstrators demanding an end to the denial of their rights in southern states. In the 1960s television broadcast the burning cities in the north with blacks protesting against high unemployment and poverty. At that time the USA was spending billions on the Vietnam War and dispatching a disproportionate number of blacks to fight it.[28]

Tariq Ali: 'City of London and US ... running this government'

In each European country where the campuses erupted in 1968 there were grievances about the way universities were run, about teaching and physical conditions on campus.[29] University structures were outmoded and the student population had expanded rapidly across Europe; in France, for example, from 123,000 in 1946 to 514,000 in 1968.[30] In all cases radical students wanted to take up political issues as well. In West Germany the student organisation SDS had been expelled from the parent organisation, the Social Democratic Party (SPD) in 1960. The SDS had since then attempted to mobilise opinion against colonialist and right-wing regimes such as South Africa, President Tshombe of Zaire and the Shah of Iran. Domestically, the big issue was opposition to proposed emergency powers legislation, which, given Germany's Nazi past, many liberals feared. When the Social Democrats joined the Christian Democrats in a coalition in 1966, led by former Nazi Kurt Georg Kiesinger, and agreed to co-operate in passing the emergency powers legislation, Germany appeared to be on a very dangerous path. In the months after the police in West Berlin killed Benno Ohnesorg during an anti-Shah demonstration in 1967, support for the SDS escalated.

In Britain, by 1968, enthusiasm for Harold Wilson's Labour government, first elected in 1964, had evaporated. The poor economic situation it inherited meant cuts in public spending. As important for the students was Wilson's public support for the USA in Vietnam and the lack of action against the rebel, racist, regime in Rhodesia. Tariq Ali, President of the Oxford Union, concluded in 1965, 'It was rapidly obvious that the City of London and the U.S. State Department were going to be running this government.'[31] Student militants demonstrated and staged occupations of university buildings at Essex University, the London School of Economics and elsewhere. It was in France, however, that the most dramatic events occurred.

1968: Cohn-Bendit, 'no longer on the people's side'

General de Gaulle was firmly in the saddle in France and appeared to be on the way to creating a Franco-style regime. At the Sorbonne in Paris right-wingers attacked a student union office on 2 May, and at the outskirts of Nanterre University Maoist students gathered to thwart a threatened right-wing attack. When Nanterre was closed by the university authorities, student militants met at the Sorbonne. In an unprecedented move, the chancellor called the police, who allowed the women to go but arrested the male students. In an apparently spontaneous reaction,[32] other students attacked the police vans carrying off their colleagues. A demonstration organised for 6 May had the backing of the university lecturers' union and older school students. When the demonstrators attempted to reach the Sorbonne riot police used teargas and truncheons to stop them. A rally on 10 May drew 20,000; after some hesitation the police again punched into the crowds. This was the bitterest night of all and became known as the 'night of the barricades'. Radio reporters were on the spot, transmitting live to all of France.

One of the key figures in this student agitation was Daniel Cohn-Bendit, a 23-year-old Nanterre sociology student born in France of German refugee parents. Backed by the Trotskyist JCR, he had a flare for media publicity. In a radio interview he threw down the challenge to the trade unions to call a strike. If they did not, 'it meant they were no longer on the people's side'.[33] The Communist, Socialist and teachers' unions were forced to oblige. A one-day strike was called for 13 May, De Gaulle's tenth anniversary in power – around a million people demonstrated through Paris. The government capitulated, withdrawing the police from the Sorbonne and releasing the detained students. In the following days the strike movement spread throughout France, involving 9 million people. It was the biggest labour revolt in French history.[34] The workers went back with promises of wage increases, a reduction in working hours and an extension of collective bargaining rights. After consulting his generals, De Gaulle decided to remain in office and call an election. The Right won the election, gaining decisively in seats but not in votes. De Gaulle revealed he was no Franco. He was gone within the year, having lost a referendum on constitutional reform. The 'May days' proved that all those on Left and Right who believed that old-style mass agitation would not happen and could not work were wrong.

The Soviet invasion of Czechoslovakia on 20 August 1968, in which reform Communists were attempting to introduce 'Socialism with a human face', was a great disappointment to left-wing students everywhere. Disillusion set in. Concessions by university authorities abolishing petty restrictions and introducing student representation on university bodies also helped to assuage student opinion. In West Germany the election of Willy Brandt as German chancellor in September 1969, in coalition with the liberal Free Democrats, marked a decisive turning point. Many felt they could now work within the system to bring about the changes they desired. A tiny handful turned to terrorism. In Britain too, many of those who led students in 1968 turned to more orthodox paths. Kim Howells, one of the prime movers of the Hornsey Art College occupation, was elected to parliament and joined the Labour government in 1997. Jack Straw, President of the National Union of Students, was elected to parliament in 1979 and was appointed home secretary in 1997. David Triesman, an Essex Maoist, was elected secretary of the Association of University Teachers. A face in the crowd at Oxford rather than a student leader, Bill Clinton was elected president of the United States in 1993. Finally, Cohn-Bendit became a German Green member of the European Parliament in the 1990s.

Chapter 6

The climax of European Social Democracy?
1969–82

1964–70: Wilson, Washington's 'sincere friend'

Harold Wilson, elected British prime minister in 1964, enjoyed a higher average popularity rating between 1964 and 1966 than any other previous prime minister. He came to office 'with the emphasis on policies that would appeal to the middle classes and those who were more concerned with national prosperity and an efficiently run economy than with abstract justice or the application of egalitarian principles'.[1] Despite the economic problems he inherited, his government increased its majority from four in 1964 to ninety-six in 1966. Yet his popularity waned rapidly after that, as his government stumbled from one crisis to another. Wilson appeared to have done no strategic planning.[2] He was not a Socialist in any real sense.[3] In his first television interview as Labour leader he said his Socialism was rooted in the Boy Scout movement.[4] He had a preference for 'order and hierarchy'[5] and was a dedicated monarchist.[6] Wilson had an inflated view of what Britain could do in the world. He had been many times to the USA and the Soviet Union before becoming prime minister, but he did not seem to understand the realities of world power. He believed fervently in Britain's imperial role and the sanctity of Commonwealth ties.[7] Henry Kissinger, US secretary of state, regarded him as 'a sincere friend' of the USA.[8] Economics rather than conviction forced Wilson to embark on a rapid retreat from Britain's global role. One legacy of Wilson that his left-wing colleagues hated was the setting up of a new defence sales department in the Ministry of Defence, headed by a private sector businessman, to boost British arms exports. It was arguably the most successful of his innovations.[9]

Having retired suddenly in 1976, under as yet unexplained circum-stances,[10] Wilson was asked by his successor to head an investigation into the working of the City of London. He came to the conservative conclusions that no serious reconstruction was required, and if it was, the City should do it itself.[11]

What were the achievements of Wilson's administration before it faced a surprise defeat by Edward Heath's Conservatives in 1970? Britain became somewhat less hierarchical, more humane and somewhat freer. The introduction of comprehensive education marginally helped this trend, as did the expansion of higher education, including the establishment of the polytechnics (1966) by Anthony Crosland. Laws against racial discrimination (1965), the less hypocritical 'no fault' divorce law of 1969, the decriminalisation of homosexual relations (1967), and the abolition of capital punishment (1965, 1969) moved the country in this direction. The Open University was established (1965), and this extended higher education to some of those who had missed out at an earlier stage in their lives. Barbara Castle's Equal Pay Act (1970) helped a minority of women indus-trial workers. Liberal David Steel's success with the Abortion Reform Act (1967) rested on the Labour majority in the Commons. The honours system was not radically changed. Nevertheless, sport, entertainment and the arts received greater recognition. The award of the MBE to the Beatles in June 1965 for 'services to exports' was symbolic of this trend. The spread of 'classless', mid-Atlantic popular culture based on the 'affluent society' conspired to this end as well. This was of course independent of politics. One other reform was the lowering of the voting age from 21 to 18 in 1969, following trends in other countries. Following trends in northern Europe, Britain appointed its first ombudsman in August 1966. This gave citizens the right to challenge the actions of public bodies.

1974–9: Labour's economic performance 'pitiable'

The Arab–Israeli Six-Day War had hit the British economy in June 1967, when Wilson was at the helm. He claimed this was the main cause of the devaluation of sterling at that time.[12] Worse was the damage caused by the Arab-Israeli War of October 1973 when Heath was prime minister. Using oil as a political weapon, Arab oil producers cut supplies, and later OPEC, which included non-Arab oil states as well, demanded massive price increases. It needs to be mentioned that the industrialised states had been exporting their inflation to the oil producers (and other commodity exporters) for years. At that time two-thirds of Britain's oil came from the Middle East. Sensing their renewed importance, the British miners banned overtime in November. They too had seen a relative decline in their incomes over the years. On 10 February 1974 the miners went on strike. The government bungled the negotiations. As future Conservative leader Margaret Thatcher was to write later, 'it looked as if we were not interested [in a settlement]'.[13]

A Conservative victory at the election of February 1974 appeared likely, as Heath campaigned on 'who governs?'[14] In fact the Conservatives won only 297 seats compared with 330 in 1970, Labour's total increased from 288 to 301, with the Liberal total going up to 14 from just 6. Turnout was up from 72 per cent to 78.8 per cent. The Conservatives were still ahead of Labour, with 37.8 per cent of the vote to Labour's 37.1. The Liberal percentage was up from 7.5 to 19.4. As the Liberals refused to back Heath, Wilson once again became the prime minister. He lost no time in settling the miners' dispute, repealing Conservative legislation restricting the unions and discontinuing their pay policy. In October Britain went to the polls again, with Labour securing a majority of three seats. This time the three parties' percentages were Labour 39.2, Conservatives 35.8 and Liberals 18.3.

Labour under Wilson and then Callaghan, from April 1976, had to face the inherited economic crisis and divisions over EEC membership. Heath's lasting legacy was to take Britain into the EEC. Wilson, himself sceptical about the EEC, held his party together by offering to renegotiate the terms and, an event unparalleled in British history, put the issue to a referendum. Much of the debate was 'phoney', as the real issue was whether or not Britain should finally join the process of European integration.[15] The new terms were rejected in the Commons by 145 Labour MPs and approved by 137 (with 33 abstaining). Conservative and Liberal MPs secured a majority for Wilson and Callaghan (foreign secretary). The Cabinet voted by sixteen to seven for staying in. In the 1975 referendum future Labour leaders Michael Foot and Neil Kinnock,[16] as well as others on the Left, joined Enoch Powell and other right-wingers to oppose Britain's EEC membership. In the end 17.5 million voters disagreed with them and only 8.5 million voted for Britain to come out. Roy Jenkins led the campaign in the Labour Party to stay in. The anti-EEC campaigners opposed

Britain limiting its sovereignty by joining a foreign body. But had it not already done so when it joined NATO, the UN, GATT and other international bodies? And did the anti-marketers not realise that Britain could not stand alone in turbulent economic conditions? Socialism could not be built on Britain's small island. If there was any chance at all for Democratic Socialism it could only be with the other parties in Europe. Foot and others had vague notions about Socialism emerging in the newly independent Commonwealth states. The overthrow of Dr Nkrumah of Ghana in 1966 was symbolic of the death of 'African Socialism'. Tony Benn believed Nkrumah had 'isolated himself from the people'.[17] One African state after another became authoritarian or a military dictatorship.

Britain's continuing poor economic situation meant that by 1976 the Labour government found itself virtually a prisoner of the International Monetary Fund (IMF). A former Labour MP summed up the economic performance of the Wilson–Callaghan government as 'pitiable. It achieved no growth, record inflation and a postwar record in unemployment.'[18] Chancellor Denis Healey was forced to go to the IMF for credit and to cut public spending, making 'nonsense' of the platform on which Labour had been elected.[19] With Liberal help the government limped on until 1979, when it was defeated by the Conservatives under Margaret Thatcher, who became Britain's first woman prime minister. She had defeated Heath in a leadership contest in 1975.

1969: Brandt led Germans 'out of master race tradition'

Gustav Heinemann (SPD) owed his one-majority election as FRG president in 1969 to the votes of the liberal FDP. Like Britain, Germany was changing. Older people who had lived through the crises of the past wanted security above all. This they had in their excellent social security system, full employment and their alliance with NATO. A minority was angry that Germany was still divided. Some feared that 'guest workers' arriving in increasing numbers could endanger their jobs. Some CDU/CSU voters felt their leaders had sold out to the 'Marxist' SPD by joining it in coalition in 1966. They turned to the NPD, founded in 1964. By 1969 this Far-Right party had managed to gain seats in the majority of regional parliaments. On the other hand, there was now a generation of voters who were not as cowed and conservative as their elders and looked rather critically on the older generation. Many young men resented being conscripted into the armed forces. Many young people were looking for more than just the prosperity that had swept across the land. Students had been turning to the FDP, the only opposition party in the Bundestag which had moved to the Left over the 1960s. Heinemann's election was a sign that the FDP was ready to join the SPD in coalition, if they could win enough seats in the 1969 election. In this hard-fought election the SPD projected itself as a modern party, a party of competence as well as of compassion. Its leaders had gained in public esteem during the years in government with the CDU/CSU. By comparison the Christian Democrats appeared old-fashioned. Yet the CDU/CSU still gained 46.1 per cent (47.6 per cent in 1965) of the votes, the SPD 42.7 per cent (39.3) and the FDP 5.8 per cent (9.5). The NPD, with 4.3 per cent, failed to gain the 5 per cent minimum necessary for parliamentary representation. It soon virtually disappeared.

On 21 October 1969, Willy Brandt was elected chancellor of the Federal Republic with the votes of the FDP. This was the first time the SPD had led a German government since 1928. Together the SPD and the FDP held 254 seats, as against 242 held by the CDU/CSU. Walter Scheel (FDP) became deputy chancellor and foreign minister. Brandt was far more popular abroad than at home. He had come to symbolise the 'good German'. His excellent command of English made him familiar to audiences in Britain and the USA. He was the first clear anti-Nazi to head a West German government. At home he had been vilified because he had left Germany in the 1930s, and attacked because of his 'illegitimate' birth. But Catholic writer Heinrich Böll summed up the feelings of many younger Germans when he wrote that Brandt was the first to lead the Germans 'out of the master race tradition'.[20]

Brandt was determined to make a breakthrough for peace with the Soviet bloc without undermining West Germany's security. France and above all the USA helped him. In France the more flexible Georges Pompidou had replaced De Gaulle. In the USA, President Nixon, to the surprise of many, was seeking détente with Moscow and Beijing. Nixon had been convinced by his secretary of state, German-Jewish-born Henry Kissinger, that Brandt was reliable.[21] After long negotiations a Treaty of Non-Aggression was signed between West Germany and the Soviet Union in August 1970. In December 1970 Brandt went to Warsaw for the signing of a similar treaty with Poland. He got widespread positive publicity for kneeling in front of a memorial at the site of the Jewish ghetto razed to the ground by the Nazis. In the meantime (March 1970) Brandt had also visited Erfurt in East Germany. There he met the GDR's head of government Willi Stoph and was surprised by a spontaneous welcome given to him by hundreds[22] of East Germans outside his hotel. Later in the year Stoph visited Kassel in West Germany. These meetings were the prelude to negotiations which ended in the Basic Treaty between the GDR and the FRG signed on 21 December 1972. This was preceded by the Quadripartite Agreement on Berlin (3 September 1971), signed by the four powers guaranteeing the security of West Berlin. Under the Basic Treaty the two German states recognised each other as equal partners, but Bonn insisted that they were not foreign to each other. The main thrust of the treaty, from Brandt's perspective, was humanitarian improvements. The East Germans saw it as a means of gaining recognition for their isolated state. Advancing by 'small steps' and (positive) 'change through rapprochement' were the phrases which summed up the big idea behind the strategy of Ostpolitik. The term 'Ostpolitik' (Eastern policy) entered the international vocabulary. Egon Bahr, author of the strategy of Ostpolitik, carried on the negotiations. In 1972 Brandt was awarded the Nobel Peace Prize. The GDR gained international recognition in the following two years. The number of West Germans visiting the GDR, often to see their relatives, increased from 1.1 million in 1969 to 2.2 million in 1973.[23] The travellers in the other direction were mainly pensioners. The Berlin Wall was opened for Western visitors. All these visitors poured millions of marks into East Germany. They also brought ideas with them, and made it more difficult for GDR propagandists to portray Bonn as a 'revanchist' state.

Brandt's majority was whittled down by defections, and fresh elections were held on 19 November 1972. They produced the highest turnout – 91.1 per cent – in the history of the FRG. For the first and only time up to 1998 the SPD gained more votes than the CDU/CSU. The SPD won 45.8 per cent, the CDU/CSU 44.9 per cent and the FDP 8.4 per cent. The lowering of the voting age to 18 helped Brandt. Estimates concluded that almost 75 per cent of 18- to 20-year-olds voted for the Brandt coalition. The election results could have been even better had not the SPD suffered from open strife. 'Star' Minister of Economics and Finance Professor Karl Schiller left the government and supported the CDU/CSU because his demands for massive public spending cuts were overruled. This ex-Nazi was heartily disliked by his colleagues, but had gained a public following for his apparent economic wizardry.

Around fifty SPD left-wingers, supporters of the so-called 'Jusos' (Young Socialists) and the Leverkusen Circle, gained seats in 1969. They hoped for changes in the direction of Socialism. At the SPD conference at Hanover in 1973 the Left was held in check by the moderates, the Kanalarbeiter, led by Egon Franke. However, they scored in appointments to the party directorate. Of thirty-four members twenty-eight had belonged to the Right; after Hanover only eight did so.[24] The Left was to be disappointed. Some of Brandt's reforms were vetoed by the FDP. However, the Plant Constitution Law (1972) considerably extended the range of matters over which management was required to consult works councils. In 1974 the FDP was persuaded to drop its opposition to extending employee co-determination rights to cover all firms (not just those in coal and steel) employing more than 2,000 persons. Other reforms to benefit the poorer members of society had to be shelved due to financial difficulties. In 1973 the way was opened for the introduction of comprehensive schools in those Länder which favoured them, and student grants and loans were introduced in 1971. No-fault divorce was also introduced in 1970. It has been argued[25] that Brandt's domestic reforms were less significant than those of the Adenauer era – co-determination in heavy industry, the indexation of pensions in 1957, or the public housing laws of the 1950s. In a sense this is true. But Adenauer's reforms were carried through with great pressure from the trade unions, the SPD and the working-class wing of the CDU.

Brandt resigned in 1974 after a personal aide, Günter Guillaume, was exposed as an East German spy. Most thought Brandt had no need to go but he was ill and depressed. His successor was the more right-wing Helmut Schmidt. A former Second World War artillery officer, he had served as minister of defence under Brandt before taking over Schiller's ministries in 1972. He had studied economics under Schiller at Hamburg University. Later they became great rivals. The Foreign Ministry went to Hans-Dietrich Genscher (FDP) who was also styled deputy chancellor. Schmidt's term of office lasted until October 1982, with elections in 1976 and 1980. After increasing its percentage vote at every election since 1957 the SPD fell back in 1976.

Schmidt's first task throughout his period of government was how best to hold his coalition together. To a degree, this conflicted

Table 6.1   Percentage votes in German federal elections 1969–83

Party	1969	1972	1976	1980	1983
CDU/CSU	46.1	44.9	48.6	44.5	48.8
SPD	42.7	44.9	42.6	42.9	38.2
FDP	5.8	8.4	7.9	10.6	7.0
Greens	–	–	–	1.5	5.6
NPD	4.3	0.6	0.3	0.2	0.2

with his attempts to keep his party behind him, for many in the SPD thought he went too far in appeasing the FDP. Schmidt's second priority was to grapple with the economic problems caused by the oil crises of 1973 and 1979 which caused the world recession of 1979–82. As elsewhere, massive public spending cuts were introduced. Internally, West Germany faced a wave of urban terrorism by the 'Red Army Faction'. The deteriorating relations between Moscow and Washington from the late 1970s onwards also put Schmidt in a difficult position. Finally all these factors helped to bring about a fracturing of political loyalties, which found expression in the rise of the Green movement. The Greens attracted many young, better-educated Protestants who opposed nuclear power, nuclear weapons and industrial growth, and campaigned for civil rights and on women's issues. Initially they grew out of the debris of the SDS and earlier protest movements starting in Lower Saxony in 1977. They achieved national parliamentary representation for the first time in the 1983 elections following Schmidt's 1982 defeat.

Austria: 'Kreisky – who else?'

Austria became one of the great success stories in postwar Europe as it gradually moved up to have one of the highest per capita incomes in the world. It benefited from its neutral status, low arms expenditure, geographical location for exports to Germany and its Soviet-bloc neighbours, and the high skills of its workforce. Its political peace and social partnership were equally important. This was based on the determination of the two main political camps, the SPÖ and the ÖVP, not to repeat the mistakes they had made in interwar Austria, which brought civil war and allowed Hitler to take over the country. This meant that changes were worked out by consensus rather than confrontation. Up to 1999 the SPÖ had only been out of government between 1966 and 1970. In the 1966 election the SPÖ lost votes to Franz Olah's splinter group, the Democratic Progressive Party, thus giving the ÖVP a majority. Between 1970 and 1983 the SPÖ was strong enough to rule the country alone, but even then most of the laws passed were agreed with the main opposition. During this period the SPÖ's leader Bruno Kreisky headed the government. Kreisky, from a wealthy Jewish family, was a prewar socialist who fled from the Nazis to Sweden in 1938. He served as foreign minister from 1959 to 1966. Under Kreisky, the SPÖ had developed from a party based largely on the working class of Vienna to a people's party covering the whole of the country. Kreisky proved very popular as an individual, so much so that in 1975 his party's electoral slogan was 'Kreisky – who else?' and in 1979 'Austria needs Kreisky.'[26] Thanks to his long involvement in international diplomacy he was able to endow Austria with an importance well beyond that justified by its size. Social partnership was based on a high level of unionisation, union representation at all levels and a centralised union federation that could enforce an incomes policy agreed with employers and government.

1981: Mitterrand's French victory

Standing for national unity, economic modernisation and an independent foreign policy, Georges Pompidou, a successful prime minister under President De Gaulle, saw off his left-wing challenger, Alain Poher, winning the French presidential election of 1969. The Left learned from this defeat. The Socialists of the SFIO remodelled themselves and with other Socialist groups set up the Socialist Party (PS). At the Épinay Congress in June 1971 the PS was enlarged and François Mitterrand, a non-Marxist and experienced minister in governments of the Fourth Republic, was elected leader. In June 1972, the PS and the Communists agreed a common programme and an electoral pact. In 1974, on the sudden death of Pompidou, Giscard d'Estaing won for the right of centre by the narrowest of margins over Mitterrand. The Gaullists were closer to the Christian Democrats in their social concerns than they were to the British Conservatives. Giscard introduced a number of reforms. He appointed a minister for women's affairs, legalised (with Socialist and Communists votes) abortion, lowered the voting age to 18, freed broadcasting from state control, introduced a capital gains tax and comprehensive schooling, and increased retirement pensions. In 1978, the divided Left lost again in the elections for the National Assembly (parliament). Fearing they would be dominated by the revamped PS, the Communists had campaigned hard as the 'true' Socialists. By the time of the presidential elections in 1981 the tide had turned. France, like Britain and Germany, had been hit by the worldwide recession. Those in office paid the price. Giscard lost to Mitterrand, who gained 51.75 per cent of the vote. To press home his success, Mitterrand called an election for the National Assembly from which the PS emerged with 37.5 per cent and 285 seats, the Communists with 16.2 per cent of the vote and 44 seats, and other left-wing parties with 2 per cent and 5 seats. The right-of-centre parties gained 43.2 per cent and 157 seats.[27] It looked as if a new age for the French Left was dawning; it looked like 1936 all over again.

1981: Papandreou attacks 'paternalistic capitalism'

In October 1981 PASOK, the Pan-Hellenic Socialist Movement, won the Greek elections with over 48 per cent of the vote. As its name suggests, PASOK sought to appeal to Greek values and patriotism. It had been a short road for PASOK but a long one for Andreas Papandreou who founded the movement in 1974. Papandreou was the son of Georgios Papandreou, a Liberal politician who had served as prime minister. Andreas Papandreou gained a PhD at Harvard University and became an American citizen. After service in the US Navy in the Second World War he worked as an academic economist teaching in Harvard, Minnesota and Berkeley. After more university work in Greece he was elected to parliament in 1964 and was appointed minister of co-ordination in a government led by his father. He was arrested when the military seized power in 1967. Due to the intervention of President Johnson, after petitioning by his former US colleagues, Papandreou, no longer a US citizen, was allowed to leave Greece. In exile in Canada and Sweden he built up what became the nucleus of PASOK.

In the 1950s Greece emerged from wartime occupation and postwar civil war with a shaky democracy and an equally shaky economy. It had a large, poor agricultural sector, an overmanned service sector and a small manufacturing sector. It was well known for its shipping magnates but their money was mainly located abroad. The apparent stability attracted foreign capital in the 1960s. A founder member of NATO, Greece was an American dependency. Greek politics continued to be dominated by fear of Turkey and, from 1945, fear of Communism. The right-wing Radical Union of Greece (ERE) dominated the political scene. The main opposition was the liberal Centre Union (EK) led by Papandreou senior. The EK won the 1964 election only to be overthrown by the military coup of 1967. The junta took power under the guise of saving the country from Communism but in reality feared the loss of its privileges if the Ministry of Defence came under parliamentary control.[28] They attempted to mobilise conservative opinion by appealing to fatherland, family and religion. By forcing the king into exile they lost any hope of monarchist support. The Americans found it easier to deal with a military than with a parliamentary democracy. Western Socialists in office in Britain, Germany and Sweden protested but did little.[29]

Within Greece opposition groups were assisted by expatriate Greek communities, which existed throughout Europe and beyond. Occasionally the junta caused widespread condemnation abroad – as when it crushed a student protest by occupying Athens Polytechnic causing thirty deaths and many wounded. Using the Nationalist card it attempted to force through the union of Cyprus and Greece in 1974. The result was a Turkish invasion of the island, which left it divided into Greek and Turkish areas. Greek impotence in the face of the Turkish invasion brought about the collapse of the regime and the return to political pluralism under the conservative politician Kostantinos Karamanlis. He made the Communist KKE, PASOK and other parties legal, drew up a constitution and initiated a referendum on the monarchy. Held on 8 December 1974, this confirmed abolition by a majority of 69 per cent.[30] Karamanlis' New Democracy won the 1974 election with 54.4 per cent against PASOK's 13.6 per cent and the KKE's 9.5 per cent. Karamanlis had fought as a Greek patriot who wanted to Europeanise his country by membership of the EEC. Protesting against NATO's lack of sanctions against Turkey he withdrew from the command structure of the alliance but like De Gaulle did not wish to withdraw from NATO altogether. Papandreou rejected both the EEC and NATO. He saw his country ensnared by American and West European 'paternalistic capitalism' and sought economic independence and a non-aligned status like that of neighbouring Yugoslavia. He called

Table 6.2   Percentage votes in Greek elections 1977–81

Party	1977	1979	1981
PASOK	13.6	25.3	48.1
KKE	9.5	9.4	10.9
ND	54.3	41.8	35.9
UC	20.4	12.0	0.4

for the nationalisation of the commanding heights of the economy and promised to build a comprehensive welfare state. He struck a chord among the electorate and in 1977 nearly doubled PASOK's percentage to 25.3. The battle for office was finally won in 1981 when PASOK attracted 48.1 per cent of the vote. The KKE stubbornly maintained its position with 10.9 per cent.

Papandreou, who was regarded almost as a god-like figure, dominated PASOK throughout the 1970s and later. He had the charisma and the rhetoric to give the Greeks a badly needed feeling of dignity. He was helped by the slump of 1980.

Soares and Gonzales

In Spain and Portugal the dictatorships still held a firm grip in the early 1970s. In Italy the Christian Democrats clung to office. But in all three there was increasing opposition to the status quo. In Spain in 1975 Franco died aged 83. In neighbouring Portugal his ideological brother, Salazar, died in 1970 aged 81. In a sense, both could claim to have been successful, if only because they had held power far longer than other European rightist dictators such as Mussolini or Hitler. They were saved by remaining neutral in the Second World War and by the US need for allies against the Soviets in the Cold War. In Spain there was also the feeling that almost anything was better than a renewed civil war. Portugal was admitted to NATO in 1948, and Spain had a pact with the USA from 1953. Their alliances, weak economies and dependence on international goodwill limited both regimes to a degree. Both were continuously harried by internal and émigré opposition. The Portuguese dictatorship was finally overthrown by a military coup, in April 1974. Portugal had attempted to defy the international trend of decolonisation and had fought colonial wars in Angola, Mozambique and

Guinea. It had not had the resources to sustain these campaigns. Elements in the armed forces recognised this. The coup led to demonstrations and strikes in favour of change. Having the best underground organisation, the Communists seemed strong initially. They joined the first provisional government. Among the exiles who returned was Mario Soares, who had co-operated with the Communists in opposition. He had been imprisoned twelve times before being exiled. With the help of the SPD and the Socialist International he re-established the Socialist Party founded in 1875 and banned in 1933. He joined the government as foreign minister. In the elections, which were held in April 1975, the Socialists surprised many by gaining 38 per cent to 12.5 per cent for the Communists and 26 per cent for the centrist Popular Democrats. The Communists had frightened many by their 'Stalinist' approach, which differed from the 'Eurocommunist' approach of the Italian, Spanish and some other Western Communist parties. After appearing to come close to civil war, Portugal settled down to being a democratic state led by Soares, who set about the painful task of transforming Western Europe's poorest, most under-educated country.

Spain's situation was very different. It had developed rapidly from the 1950s onwards, fuelled by tourism, remittances from migrant Spaniards abroad and, later on, increasing foreign invest- ment. The state created major industries and the industrial working class was greatly expanded. Agricultural employment fell from 42 per cent to 18 per cent between 1960 and 1980.[31] Between 1960 and 1967 over 1.8 million workers emigrated to other European states.[32] Although there were instances of brutal repression, industrial unrest and political agitation grew over the 1960s and 1970s. The dictatorship was limited by Spain's desire to be part of Europe. From 1967 it was possible to find publications of all varieties of Marxism in Spain, and the degree of ideological sophistication that existed within the Spanish Left was easily comparable with any other European society.[33] Franco had proclaimed Spain a monarchy; Juan Carlos was groomed to be king and took over on Franco's death. Initially he was backed by Franco's supporters, which made it easier for him to steer a course towards democracy before they realised what was happening. Early in 1977 political parties and trade unions were legalised and on 15 June the first free elections since 1936 were held. The Socialists (PSOE) gained 29 per cent of the vote, the Communists 9 per cent, the Popular Alliance (associated with former Francoists) 8 per cent and the UDC, an amalgam of Christian Democrats and other centre moderates, 35 per cent. In December 1978 a new constitution was approved by 90 per cent of the voters in a referendum. It included commitments to health, the right to work and a fair distribution of wealth, as well as enshrining the traditional liberal democratic rights. The monarchy was reduced to a largely ceremonial role, there was no state Church and the regions were promised 'the right to self-government'. Juan Carlos was given the chance to show his democratic credentials when military plotters seized the parliament in 1981. He appealed to the armed forces to remain loyal to the constitution, which they did. In elections held in 1982 the Socialists secured 46 per cent of the vote, giving them an absolute majority in the Cortes. The UDC slumped to 7 per cent and the Popular Alliance rose to 26 per cent. Felipe Gonzalez, a 40-year-old charismatic lawyer, who transformed the PSOE from a Marxist party into a pragmatic one, took over as prime minister – a post he was to occupy until 1996. Spain's transition to democracy was possible because most Spaniards of all parties wanted to be part of mainstream Europe, the European Community. This was only possible if they embraced democracy. They also had a great dread of another civil war.

'Eurocommunism' and the State

Franco continually stressed the 'Communist threat', making the Communists appear far stronger than they were, but even they had learned from the past. Their leader, Santiago Carrillo, wrote in his *'Eurocommunism' and the State* (1976): 'In the struggle against fascism we communists ... have confirmed that democratic liberties, even with all the limitations imposed in bourgeois society, have a real value which must not be underestimated.'[34] He denounced the 'dictatorship of the proletariat' as 'not the way in the democratic countries of developed capitalism'.[35] He denied that the Soviet Union was a 'genuine workers' democracy' but claimed that it was subject to a 'bureaucratic stratum'.[36] He also emphasised his party's independence from Moscow and denounced the Soviet occupation of Czechoslovakia as the 'straw that broke the camel's back'.[37] He was not saying that force was never legitimate in the struggle for freedom, and he recognised that even in seemingly democratic states a left-wing government could be overthrown by force – as in Chile in 1973.

Carrillo's ideas found echoes in the British, French, Italian and other Western Communist parties. At conferences in 1976 and 1977 and in declarations they asserted their independence from the Soviet Union and their adherence to Western democratic values. It was the Italians who had gone farthest over a comparatively longer period. As the figures below reveal, the PCI maintained its position as the main challenger to the DC up to the 1980s. It could do this because, despite immense progress, Italy was still very much a divided society. Workers felt that they were not really sharing in the growing affluence. Like the Catholic Church, the PCI offered a wide range of services to its members; as in the pre-Hitler SPD, they could live an 'alternative life' once they left their workplace. This helped to sustain membership, particularly in core strongholds. The PCI also attempted to overcome 'sectarian tendencies'. It sought, for instance, to avoid religious controversy that might isolate Communists. It was helped by the declining influence of the Church. From 1956 onwards the PCI increasingly voiced its independence of Moscow and its view that the Soviet model was not its model. Under Enrico Berlinguer, leader 1972–84, the PCI reversed its earlier opposition to the EEC and even accepted Italian membership of NATO in 1975. Influenced by events in Chile, where the democratically left-wing government had been overthrown by the military, he also proclaimed the 'historic compromise' (1973) between the PCI, the DC and other democratic parties, ensuring Communist co-operation in the functioning and maintenance of Italian democracy. This democracy was under attack from left- and right-wing terrorism. Unexpectedly, Sandro Pertini, an elderly Socialist, was elected president in 1978 (to 1985), and he did much to revive respect for institutions and to encourage popular counteraction not only against terrorism but against the mafia and the widespread corruption in politics.[38] What of his Socialist Party?

When the DC had attempted, in 1960, to rule with the support of the Far Right, massive protest had erupted. The DC was forced to turn left and agreed, in 1963, to a broad coalition including the Socialists, who were now respectable as they had distanced themselves from the PCI in 1958 over entry into the EEC. In 1961 Nenni accepted NATO and in 1963 his party entered the DC-led government, remaining in office throughout the 1960s. This caused a party split in 1964 when a group headed by Lelio Basso left to form the PSIUP. Attempts were then made to reunite with the PSDI but these failed. Moreover, the DC did not deliver on any promised

Table 6.3 Percentage votes in elections to Italian Chamber of
Deputies 1963–83

Party	1963	1968	1972	1976	1979	1983
PCI	25.3	26.9	27.1	34.4	30.4	29.9
PSI	13.8		9.6	9.6	9.8	11.4
PSDI	6.1	14.5*	5.1	3.4	3.8	4.1
Republicans	1.4	2.0	2.9	3.1	3.0	5.1
DC	38.3	39.1	38.7	38.7	38.3	32.9
Liberal Party	7.0	5.8	3.9	1.3	1.9	2.9
Right/MSI	6.8	5.7	8.7	6.1	5.3	6.8

Source: Adapted from Ginsborg (1989: 442)

Note: * In 1968 the PSI and the PSDI stood together as the PSU.

reforms except for the nationalisation of electricity. Divided and
losing support, the Socialists opted to steer clear of government from
1972 to 1980. Elected in 1976 as PSI leader, Bettino Craxi decided
his party needed to be more critical of the PCI if it was to have a
major impact. By 1983 Craxi's clever manoeuvring put him at the
head of a five-party government – a government which proved to be
the longest lasting since 1944.

The challenge of 'embourgeoisement'

What had European Socialist parties become by the early 1980s in
terms of their membership, sociology, programmes and ideals? In
France, the PS increased its membership from 80,300 in 1971 to
192,000 in 1979. Its 1981 success led to a further expansion.[39] Its
rival, the PCF, claimed around 750,000 members in 1980, more than
double the membership of 1974. PS membership was small by
German SPD standards. The SPD had boasted over one million
members in 1976. Membership then gently declined to 926,000 in
1982.[40] The Austrian SPÖ was even more successful in recruiting
members. Membership stood at 716,340 in 1979, an astonishing
number given the total population was only 7.5 million.[41] In both
the Austrian and German cases the high membership was based on
traditionally good organisation, which was far better than that of

either the PS or the British Labour Party. Another factor was that party membership in those countries was often important for public sector jobs, and in both countries there were many such appointments. In Vienna 40.37 per cent of Socialist voters were also SPÖ members in 1979.[42] It was rumoured that some people there were secretly members of *both* main parties. In Spain, patronage was used to buy loyalty. It has been estimated that about 50,000 public posts were given to PSOE members between 1982 and 1984. The party had around 150,000 members.[43] The number of individual members, as opposed to trade union-affiliated members, of the British Labour Party was low. Unlike many continental parties, Labour offered its members little more than occasional meetings. Members were often those seeking election to local authorities, a smattering of young idealists, those delegated from local trade unions or those recruited en masse to support an ambitious ethnic brother. The big Communist parties also attracted office seekers. Apart from the Communist Party apparatus, these parties ran businesses, satellite organisations and local authorities. In parts of France, Italy, Portugal and Spain social pressure helped recruitment and retention of members. This is a factor which applies in all significant political parties, significant enough, that is, to dominate certain regions, towns or cities. To be sure, Socialist and Communist parties everywhere still attracted young idealists and others who thought it was fashionable to join at a particular time, which was likely to be when the party was in the ascendancy.

The European Socialist parties had to face the fact that their old clientele, the industrial working class, was in decline. Jobs were being lost in manufacturing, agriculture and mining, and the service industries were expanding. This meant more carers, petrol pump cashiers, computer programmers, technicians, social workers and teachers. Socialist parties had to present themselves as broad national parties (or 'catch-all' parties) and not just as parties representing the old, male-dominated working class. A process of 'embourgeoisement' was taking place. In the SPD, the PS, PSOE, the Labour Party, the SPÖ and the other Socialist parties the parliamentary wing and the higher echelons had few manual workers. Teachers, journalists, lawyers and public sector administrators and managers were heavily represented.[44]

Although women were becoming more active in the workplace and politically aware, they were still greatly under-represented in the ranks of the Socialist parties and in parliaments. In Austria 32 per cent of members were women in 1929, 35.5 per cent in 1945, but only 33.9 per cent (of an admittedly larger party) in 1979.[45] In percentage terms, the Nordic states were electing more women to parliament than the other Western European countries in the 1970s.[46] West Germany was sending roughly double the number of women to parliament that Britain was. In Britain Labour consistently elected more women MPs than the Conservatives, except in 1970 and 1983 when the Conservatives won the elections. In 1983 the Norwegian Labour Party was the first major Social Democratic party to adopt quotas, requiring 40 per cent of all party posts to be filled by women.[47]

The leftist prime ministers of Britain, France and Norway had good records in appointing women as ministers. Women tended to be appointed to 'women's' ministries like youth and family affairs, but Wilson broke new ground by appointing Barbara Castle minister of transport in 1965. Schmidt appointed Maria Schlei as minister for economic co-operation in 1976 and under the PS in France Edwige Avice was appointed secretary of state for defence in 1984. In Norway Gro Harlem Brundtland served as minister for the environment 1974–9, leader of the Labour Party 1981–92 and head of government 1981, 1986–9 and from 1990.

Another important factor in the development of all political parties since 1945 has been the increasing role of the electronic media. Traditionally, Socialist parties had relied heavily on their own press to get their message across. From the 1930s onwards radio started to play an important role in politics. The party press remained important, however, especially where left-wing parties had little access to radio. By the late 1950s and early 1960s marketing strategies and television started to play a decisive part. The nature of television put a premium on good images rather than good arguments. Investigation of the famous Kennedy–Nixon debates in the 1960 US presidential election revealed that those who heard them on radio thought Nixon won, while those who saw them on television preferred Kennedy.[48]

Increasingly, parties had to choose leaders who could appeal to the mass television audience rather than those who were just good at stirring the party faithful. Wilson, Callaghan, Brandt, Schmidt, Kreisky, Mitterrand and later Gonzalez all fitted this requirement. These leaders were often much more popular than their parties. This gave the leader more power within the party, as mass membership was becoming less important for winning elections. The party press also became far less significant and declined to a shadow of its former self over the 1960s and beyond. Television gave the leader the opportunity to reach out far beyond his or her party's traditional supporters. This too influenced the message. It needed to be vaguer, less specific and appeal to the less political 'floating voters'. Traditionally, conservative parties had been less programme-orientated, and had closer ties to business and advertising. All this was hard for most Socialist parties to swallow and initially parties such as Labour (1959) and the SPD (1957) lost out by mounting old-fashioned campaigns. There were dangers in the new 'image-building' strategies. Party leaders could lose touch with their traditional supporters and with their party activists. This happened to Wilson, to Callaghan during the 'winter of discontent' of 1978, and to Schmidt.

Chapter 7

The Soviet Empire

Stagnation under Brezhnev, 1964–82

1964: The world held its breath

The world held its breath on 15 October 1964. In a palace coup in Moscow Khrushchev had been replaced by Leonid Brezhnev as first secretary of the CPSU. The following day the world held its breath again as it heard that China had become a nuclear power. Brezhnev, aged 58, a steel engineer by training and a party functionary by profession, had clawed his way up the party ladder with Khrushchev's help. Brezhnev was formal head of state but it was from his vantage point as secretary in charge of day-to-day CPSU affairs that he had brought down his predecessor. His position had given him the power of patronage. Alexei Kosygin replaced Khrushchev as head of government. Khrushchev had been 'an arbitrary and unpredictable leader'.[1] His foreign policy, especially with regard to the Cuban crisis and the breach with China, had worried his colleagues. His anti-Stalin campaign frightened them even more. Where would it all end? It could jeopardise increasing numbers of the party and security officials by questioning their actions during the Stalin years and the methods they still used to maintain power.

Khrushchev had at least stopped the mass liquidations of rivals, enemies and supposed enemies, and there was no going back on that. The leading role of the CPSU in the one-party state was to be maintained. Within the CPSU democratic centralism was to remain the method by which those at the top ruled over those at the bottom. Their right to do so was based on the pseudo-ideology of Marxism-Leninism and the constant appeal for vigilance against the internal and external threat of world imperialism. This justified the massive military and security apparatus. It also justified the severe limitations on any kind of individual freedom. All of this was in turn justified by reference to protecting the 'achievements of Socialism'. In the Soviet Union the state owned most industry, and what it did not directly own was in the possession of regional and city authorities. The agricultural sector was mostly divided into state and 'co-operative' farms. In fact, the Soviet economy was a vast bureaucracy based on nepotism and corruption. It was an economy based on shortage, in which the black market was normal and living standards remained low. Matters were to get much worse under Brezhnev.

Solzhenitsyn: 'A true helper of the Party'

One thing that would trouble Brezhnev far more than Khrushchev was opposition from 'dissidents'. These were loyal Communists who sought democratisation of the CPSU and greater intellectual freedom. They regarded these as part and parcel of Socialism and necessary to solve the increasing problems of a technological age. There were 'liberals' who went farther and demanded a multi-party state. Some just fought for free trade unions, others for civil rights. There were members of the surviving religious communities who demanded religious freedom and there were nationalists who wanted greater freedom for their states or complete independence. Increasingly dissidents throughout the Soviet bloc cited the Helsinki Final Act to demand their rights. This was the agreement concluded at Helsinki in 1975 by the heads of thirty-five states including the Soviet Union and the United States. It set out certain agreed principles of sovereignty, self-determination and recognition of existing frontiers. It also covered economic and technological co-operation, security, disarmament and human rights.

Solzhenitsyn's book about the labour camps was published in 1962. It was a sensation. Many wrongly believed it was the start of a new age in the Soviet Union. Its author was praised in the Soviet paper *Izvestia* as a 'true helper of the Party in a sacred and vital cause – the struggle against the personality cult and its consequences'.[2] This was in 1962 at the time of the twenty-second Congress of the CPSU, when Khrushchev was seeking popularity by showing his anti-Stalin credentials. By March 1963 Khrushchev himself was tightening up the control of the arts, demanding that artists and writers abide 'unswervingly' by the party line.[3] Once Khrushchev was deposed, the situation of writers rapidly deteriorated. Solzhenitsyn was guaranteed a certain immunity because he had become an overnight celebrity abroad. In 1969 he was expelled from the Soviet Writers Union following his book *Cancer Ward*. By January 1974 he was expelled from the Soviet Union, his own country and the land of his birth. He was welcomed in Brandt's Germany. In a way, he was lucky. In the most brutal blow[4] struck by Brezhnev against literature, the writers Andrei Sinyavsky and Yuri Daniel were sentenced to hard labour just before the twenty-third Congress of the CPSU held in March/April 1966. They had allowed their work to be published abroad and were accused of anti-Soviet propaganda. It looked as if the Soviet Union was returning to the winter of Stalin but at the congress Stalin was passed over in silence. Nevertheless Brezhnev took on the title of general secretary used by Stalin. Throughout the Soviet bloc life got harder for intellectuals. In the Soviet Union the KGB, the reorganised (1954) Soviet internal security and foreign intelligence agency, worked overtime again.

Ceausescu: 'Great Genius of the Carpathians'

In 1968 fear of loosening the reins of power resulted in the Warsaw Pact invasion of Czechoslovakia, where Communists wanting democracy within their own party and healthy debate in the media had replaced the Stalinists. Unlike the situation in Hungary in 1956 there was little violence and no blood purge later. Party control was reasserted in full. In Hungary itself, the repression of the 1950s had given way to a lighter touch by the early 1960s. The survivors of 1956 were released from prison and Kadar attempted to improve the economy whilst backing Soviet foreign policy initiatives.

Neighbouring Romania became something of a curiosity. There Nicolae Ceausescu, at 43 the youngest of the East European party bosses, had taken over after the death of Gheorghiu-Dej in 1965. Brezhnev had nothing to fear with regard to Ceausescu's internal regime becoming an alternative variety of Soviet 'Socialism'. Ceausescu and his wife Elena ran the country as their personal estate, living in great luxury. He became head of state in 1967, and in 1969 supreme military commander. To build up support he emphasised Romanian nationalism. Among his extravagant titles was 'Great Genius of the Carpathians'.[5] Was this for the way he persecuted the Hungarian minority in Romania? In foreign policy he asserted his nation's independence from the Soviet Union without, however, attempting to leave the Warsaw Pact. He did not support the invasion of Czechoslovakia, did not break diplomatic ties with Israel in 1967 after the Six-Day War, and kept up good relations with China. He was more than welcome in Western capitals and Western bankers were happy to provide credit.

Bulgaria's Todor Zhivkov followed the Soviet line in both internal and external policy. He had been helped to power by Khrushchev and a few months after his Soviet backer's fall there was a coup attempt to unseat him. This failed and he remained in office until 1989. Another curiosity was tiny Albania, the poorest country in Europe, where Enver Hoxha, son of a Muslim land-owning family and wartime partisan, ruled as a self-proclaimed Stalinist until his death in 1985. He had received Chinese backing when he challenged Khrushchev but later fell out with Beijing after its rapprochement with the USA.

1980: Gdansk 'demands' do not 'threaten the foundations of Socialism'

In contrast with the other 'Socialist states' Poland remained turbulent. Riots in 1970 brought down Gomulka, who had disappointed the masses over the years since 1956. The rise in food prices two weeks before Christmas ignited the flames in the Baltic towns. Gomulka had left Poland a littler freer than when he took office in 1956. The low point of his rule came in 1968 when he gave in to anti-Semitic elements, the so-called 'Partisans', whose activities forced many Jewish intellectuals to leave Poland. The high point came shortly before his fall when he welcomed Brandt to Warsaw to recognise Poland's Western frontier. 'Technocrat' Eduard Gierek, who replaced Gomulka, promised a reversal of the austerity programme and the modernising of the ailing economy. Gierek was aided by Western loans to build factories, which often produced Western goods, for example Peugeot cars, under licence. This had been tried with varying results around the world. The Polish economy was badly hit by the world oil crises, and by corruption and incompetence. In 1976 there was another upheaval as Gierek attempted to introduce massive price increases. Once again the price increases were rescinded but strike leaders were sacked. Among them was Lech Walesa, an electrician at the Lenin shipyard in Gdansk. In response to these events, Warsaw intellectuals Jacek Kuron and Adam Michnik formed the Committee for the Defence of Workers' Rights (KOR).

An 'accident' of considerable significance was the election of Karol Wojtyla, Cardinal Archbishop of Krakow, as Pope John Paul II in October 1978. In bad times, and especially when they were being suppressed as a nation, the Poles clung to the Catholic Church to help maintain their nationality. The Church also acted as a conduit through which Poles could have their requests and grievances passed on to the civil authorities. The Poles had an increased sense of pride that one of their own had been elected pope and that now more than ever they had a powerful ally on their side. This was evident when John Paul visited his native country in 1979. Undoubtedly, the support of the Church played a part in their renewed determination to fight for their rights. Some believed the fate of the Communist system, at least in Poland, was sealed by the papal visit.

Confrontation flared up again in July 1980 when the government announced huge food price increases. Walesa was called back by his former colleagues at the Gdansk shipyard to lead the strike committee. The strikes spread and Gierek was forced to send in a negotiator. The talks were broadcast live over a public address system. Among the many demands made by the strikers were the right to free trade unions, the right to strike and freedom of the press. The strikers reassured the Communists that 'Our demands are intended neither to threaten the foundations of the Socialist regime in our country nor its position in international relations.'[6] The government gave in to all the demands. It then used a delaying tactic to whittle down its concessions. After a heart attack Gierek was replaced by Stanislaw Kania. The union Solidarity was registered, which made it legal, on 10 November 1980. Within months it had over 9.5 million members out of a workforce of 12.5 million.[7]

After Soviet criticism, the Communists replaced Kania with Defence Minister General Jaruzelski, who became head of their party in July 1981. Meanwhile, at Solidarity's congress in September 1981, Walesa was under fire for being too timid. The truth was that Walesa realised that Solidarity could not take power. Had it tried to, the country would have faced Soviet invasion. Solidarity was able to force through industrial 'self-government' in the same month. In a situation of rapid economic decline, with Solidarity appearing to be inching its way to power, Jaruzelski proclaimed a 'state of war' on 12 December 1981. Solidarity and KOR were banned and their leaders arrested. Gierek was also among the 10,000 or so arrested.[8] A number of deaths occurred as the army seized control of strike centres. Criticised by the Catholic Church and the outside world, Jaruzelski ruled without too much repression. Walesa and some others were released in November 1982. Private negotiations between John Paul and Jaruzelski led to the lifting of martial law in 1983.

Honecker's 'Politbureau dictatorship'

Honecker's GDR remained an enigma for many in the West. Because this was, after all, Germany many were inclined to believe its boasts about its 'social achievements' in health, education and welfare.[9] The fact was it was living on the capital it had inherited and things were getting more run down. It boasted about the kindergartens it provided so that women were free to go out to work. The truth was that women were compelled to join the labour force and the conditions in the kindergartens often left much to be desired. Unlike the Czechs, Poles and Hungarians, who could visit the West, its people were walled in. Travel, even within the Soviet bloc, was limited. For a variety of reasons, individuals continued to risk their lives attempting to escape. The absence of mass demonstrations and strikes misled outsiders about the real situation. The GDR had a massive security service, the Stasi, which employed, per 10,000 of population, far more officials than Hitler's Gestapo.[10] It also recruited masses of informers. Dissidents were arrested and imprisoned and later 'bought free' by West Germany. The case of Rudolf Bahro in 1977 was just one of many. Bahro, an SED official, had allowed his book *The Alternative* to be published by a West German trade union publisher. What the SED and the Stasi found impossible to control were the ideas from the West, which entered the GDR via West German television and West German visitors. The GDR attempted to win friends and influence people through its sporting achievements and through its culture. At the Olympics in Mexico (1968), Munich (1972) and Montreal (1976) the GDR revealed itself as a world power in sports. At Montreal it actually gained more gold medals than the USA. This was achieved by careful selection of potential winners, sending them to special schools at an early age and, not least, by extensive use of drugs. The GDR thought this success would improve its image at home and abroad, and gain it influence in the Third World, whose sportsmen and women it offered to train. Its own people had far fewer facilities than West Germans or the British, and many East Germans resented the lavish expenditure in this area. Economically the GDR was regarded as the Soviet bloc's most modern economy. Due to the shortages everywhere it had no problem in selling its goods to its East European neighbours. To gain Western currency it even sold some of its consumer goods very cheaply to the West. It was also assisted by West German funds.

Bahro criticised Honecker's 'Politbureau dictatorship' which was 'a grotesque exaggeration of the bureaucratic principle. ... The whole structure is quasi-theocratic.'[11] By 1981 the average age of the SED politburo was 62.9. Honecker himself was 69, his minister of defence was 71 and his minister for state security was 74. They were more cut off from the people they ruled than almost any other elite in the world. They were of course typical of the elites of the Soviet bloc. All the top men – Honecker as well as Ceausescu – indulged in a cult of personality. In the mid-1970s there seemed to be a 'cult of personality' around Brezhnev who became a marshal of the Soviet Union, as Stalin had done, and head of state, as well remaining CPSU boss. Brezhnev died in office in 1982. He had been very ill for years. He left behind a politburo of septuagenarians and a country and an empire facing economic stagnation and social decay.

Chapter 8

Democratic Socialism in retreat

1982–92

1981: Reagan, Soviet 'evil empire'

In January 1981 the personable Ronald Reagan was inaugurated as president of the United States. He remained president until 1989. With only 53 per cent of the electorate voting, the Republican Reagan had beaten the Democrat incumbent, Jimmy Carter. Reagan, vigorous and charming despite his 69 years, had risen via Hollywood to be governor of California. He had been elected on a right-wing agenda of cutting the federal administration and reducing taxes with the money saved. This it was claimed would put more money in people's pockets so they could spend more and invest more, thus creating more jobs. Reagan targeted welfare spending. On the other hand, he immediately embarked on a defence build-up. Under Reagan defence expenditure increased in real terms by 40 per cent.[1] The arms industry became the leading growth industry. However, cuts in non-defence expenditure fell well short of target. Following the tax cuts the federal deficit soared. Under Reagan the USA became a net debtor for the first time since 1914. On 19 October 1987, 'Black Monday', a fall on Wall Street led to world-wide panic. Overnight share prices fell dramatically. The immediate cause had been a set of disappointing US trade figures. The crash brought into focus underlying concerns about the persistent US trade and budget deficits, which Reagan had made worse.[2]

Abroad, his aim was to get tough with those he identified as enemies of the USA, such as Libya, Syria, the rebels in El Salvador, the Sandinista regime in Nicaragua and former ally General Noriega in Panama. In the case of the Islamic Republic of Iran fighting one of the major wars of the twentieth century against Iraq, Reagan helped *both* sides. The Iranians bought American arms at inflated prices through Israel and other channels. Some of the profits were used to fund the Contras, guerrillas fighting the Sandinistas. Iraq received vital intelligence information from the Americans.[3] Reagan soon let it be known that he regarded the Soviet Union as the 'evil empire'. Luckily for the world, Mikhail Gorbachev took over the leadership in Moscow. He sought agreement with the West. More will be said about Reagan–Gorbachev relations in the next chapter. 'Reaganomics' and being tough with those perceived as enemies found favour with Margaret Thatcher in Britain, and influenced governments throughout the non-Communist world. Social Democracy, whether in office or out, had to contend with these trends in the 1980s.

1981: PASOK's *Contract with the People*

As we saw in Chapter 6, Papandreou won the 1981 election and for the first time Greece had a Socialist government. PASOK's election manifesto was called *A Contract with the People* and was a watered-down version of earlier policy pledges.[4] PASOK now promised a gradual removal of US bases rather than the earlier commitment to immediate withdrawal. Under an agreement negotiated in 1983 the Americans retained the bases until 1988. However, in 1987 that deadline too was lifted. The commitment to withdrawal from NATO was also dropped. In January 1981, under the previous government, Greece had joined the EEC. A promised referendum did not take place. Instead the Socialist government renegotiated the terms. Gradually, PASOK came to recognise the benefits of EEC membership. Greece was a net receiver of funds from the EEC. Countries like Britain, Germany, Italy and the Netherlands were net payers.

PASOK modernised the framework of Greek civil liberties. It legalised civil marriage, abolished the institution of dowry, established equal rights for children born outside marriage, liberalised divorce, decriminalised adultery and introduced sex equality legislation. It abolished selective secondary education, set up day-care centres and introduced paternal leave as well as maternal leave. Margaret Papandreou, Andreas' first wife, pushed this forward.[5] The PASOK government was responsible for a National Health Service Act that included rural health centres. It also challenged the Orthodox Church over its massive landholding. In a similar way to Mitterrand's administration in France, PASOK sought to spend its way out of the recession of the early 1980s. Public sector employment increased, as did wages. Unemployment was below the European average. The public debt 'skyrocketed'.[6] A stabilisation programme followed in 1985, which included limitations on the right to strike, anti-inflationary measures and devaluation. One other problem was corruption. The Papandreou government became infected by it just as earlier Greek governments had been.

The election of June 1989 produced a stalemate. New Democracy gained 145 seats to PASOK's 125, but failed to get an overall majority. After some embarrassed negotiations New Democracy formed a coalition with the Alliance of the Left and Progress, made up of the hard line and Eurocommunists. They were united on only one thing: wresting power from Papandreou. They set themselves the task of investigating the scandals and prising state-run television from the hands of pro-PASOK elements. A second election in the autumn changed little. New Democracy and PASOK gained three seats each. The Communists lost seven due to the anger and disappointment of their followers, who could not stomach the coalition with New Democracy. More remarkable was the coalition that followed, which comprised all three parties. A third election in April 1990 produced a narrow victory for New Democracy. Papandreou had a personal victory in January 1992 when an Athens court found him not guilty of corruption. The former finance minister, Dmitris Tsovolas, *was* found guilty and sent to prison. Rightly or wrongly PASOK supporters believed the trial to be politically motivated.

The New Democracy government improved relations with the USA, with Greece making a small but symbolic contribution to the Allies in the Gulf War. Hostility to Turkey continued with no end to the Cyprus problem in sight. Another problem arose on the northern frontier with the disintegration of Yugoslavia. Macedonia, formerly part of Communist Yugoslavia, became independent and was internationally recognised. Greece objected to the use of the name, fearing that the new state would seek a Greater Macedonia at the expense of parts of Greece and Bulgaria. Internally New Democracy introduced massive cuts in public spending, and increased direct and indirect taxes. This resulted in widespread strikes and a swing back to PASOK. In October 1993 that party was returned to office, winning 170 seats in contrast with 111 for New Democracy, 10 for the nationalist Political Spring Party, and 9 for the Communists. Papandreou was once again prime minister. The dispute with Greece's neighbours rumbled on, and in February 1994

Greece closed its frontier with Macedonia. The EC Commission then took Greece to the European Court of Justice.

1983: Mitterrand's U-turn

In the long years of opposition the PS had moved to the left. Three factors had brought this about. First, the fact that it had been out of office for so long and had little experience of the art of the possible. Second, the need to attract the activists of 1968. Third, there was the challenge of the PCF on its left. Although the PCF had lost support under Georges Marchais, having supported the Soviet invasion of Afghanistan and the suppression of Solidarity in Poland, it remained a strong political force.

In 1981 PS candidate François Mitterrand was rewarded for his persistency. He was elected president of the Fifth French Republic at the third attempt. He had failed against De Gaulle in 1965 and against Giscard in 1974. This time he defeated Giscard, gaining 51.8 per cent of the vote on the second ballot. The turnout was lower than in 1974, but at 86 per cent was very respectable. Mitterrand moved quickly, appointing Pierre Mauroy prime minister of a government which included Communists for the first time since 1947. Mauroy announced a package of populist reforms, raising welfare benefits by more than 20 per cent and the minimum wage by 10 per cent. But he needed a majority in the National Assembly to carry these measures through. This he won in the June elections. The PS and MRG (Left Radicals) won 286 seats, more than doubling their previous total on the second ballot. The Communists, many of whose candidates had stood aside to give the PS a clear run, won 44. The moderate Right took the other 144 seats.

The Mauroy government pushed through a radical programme which increased the state's share in banking from 70 per cent to 95 per cent and took over several of France's largest industrial groups. The public sector increased from about 8 per cent to about 25 per cent of French industrial capacity.[7] Representatives of labour took up one-third of the seats on the boards of the nationalised industries. This programme proved costly, especially after the Constitutional Council declared compensation terms inadequate and increased them by 28 per cent.[8] Mauroy's government attempted to reflate the economy Keynesian-style, increasing public spending by 28 per cent in 1981. There was help for school leavers, more civil service jobs, soft loans for private firms, an ambitious house-building programme, and more public investment targeting the high-technology sector. Taxes on tobacco, motoring and high incomes and the doubling of the public sector deficit were meant to absorb the costs. The hoped for reduction in unemployment was also meant to boost revenue. A stock market collapse, an investment strike by French private industrialists and a fall in the franc exchange rate hit the programme. Abroad, Mauroy's government was defeated by the recession spreading across the world. At the G7 summit of the leading industrial states in June 1982 the Reaganite Americans refused to lower interest rates to stimulate Western economies. Increased competition from Asia was also hitting the French and other European economies. Jacques Delors, the finance minister, soon attempted to persuade Mitterrand and his colleagues to go into reverse. By June 1982 spending cuts had followed, and a year later a third currency devaluation and a major deflationary austerity programme were introduced. This represented a humbling U-turn for Mitterrand, Mauroy and their colleagues. As unemployment rose, Mitterrand's popularity ratings fell to the lowest level for a president of the Fifth Republic.[9]

Mitterrand's first term was reforming in other directions. He abolished the death penalty and the (secret) State Security Court, improved the legal aid system, abandoned a scheme to introduce computerised identity cards, licensed free radio stations, improved the treatment of immigrant workers, reduced the working week, with five weeks paid holidays a year, and introduced voluntary retirement at the age of 60 on half pay.[10] These measures brought France more in line with its German and Scandinavian neighbours. In 1982 a law decentralised the administration, giving local and regional authorities more power.

In July 1984 the PCF withdrew its ministers from the government, having criticised both its domestic and foreign policies for some time. It had been losing support, especially among its younger followers. Mitterrand restructured the government, replacing Mauroy with Laurent Fabius, a 37-year-old former financial civil servant from a wealthy Jewish family. Delors left to take over the presidency of the EEC Commission. Tension mounted within the PS between the 'realists' such as Mitterrand, Delors and the PS General Secretary Lionel Jospin, and the Mauroy group which took a more traditional Socialist position. Further left was Jean-Pierre Chevènement, former industry minister, and his CERES faction. Finally, Michel Rocard wanted to close the door on any future alliance with the PCF and seek alliances to the right on the basis of the revised economic strategy. The PS congress of Toulouse in 1985 represented a major landmark in that theory caught up with practice. The PS recognised itself as a gradualist Social Democratic reform party rather than as a party seeking a rapid break with capitalism.[11] But it refused to countenance coalitions with the Right and did not exclude alliances with the PCF. Thus it followed the Mitterrand/Jospin/Fabius line.

The changes in the PS did not bring it a renewal of support among the public, and in 1986 it faced defeat in the elections to the National Assembly. The moderate Right's victory would have been greater had not the National Front (FN) taken votes from it. The FN had grown up since 1983, feeding on unrest over unemployment and a traditional racist spectre which haunted French politics from time to time. In 1982, 8 per cent of the population was immigrant. The biggest single group (34 per cent) came from North Africa.[12] It was easy for FN leader Jean-Marie Le Pen to raise a cheer by calling for compulsory repatriation. In the 1986 election the FN shocked many at home and abroad by gaining 10 per cent of the vote. Helped by PR, which Mitterrand had introduced, it gained 35 of the 577 seats, as many as the PCF.

On the Right some called for Mitterrand's resignation, claiming

Table 8.1   Percentage votes in elections to French National Assembly 1958–86 (first ballot)

Year	Far Left	PCF	PS/MRG	Centre	UDF	Gaullists	Far Right
1958	–	19	16	42	–	20	3
1962	2	22	13	25	6	32	1
1967	2	23	19	13	6	35	1
1968	5	21	17	11	5	38	2
1973	4	21	21	13	11	27	3
1978	3	21	25	–	20	22	3
1981	1	16	38	–	19	21	3
1986	1	10	32	–	44*		10

Source: Derbyshire (1986: 18)

Notes: * A coalition of several right-of-centre groups

it had been a plebiscite on his presidency. But the president decided to 'cohabit' with a right-of-centre government under Jacques Chirac. This was the first time that the president of the Fifth Republic was of a different political colour from the government. Under Article 5 of the constitution the president was responsible for foreign and defence policy. He could also make his 'reservations' known about aspects of domestic policy under Article 10. Chirac and Mitterrand fought each other over a number of issues and usually the prime minister, not the president, won. Chirac carried through a rapid privatisation programme, including undertakings nationalised by de Gaulle in 1947. He introduced computerised identity cards, and gave the police more powers against illegal immigrants and suspected terrorists. However, Chirac was defeated by massive protests in his attempt to restrict entry into higher education, to restrict the granting of French citizenship and in his attempts to privatise the prison service. These proposals Mitterrand had opposed.[13] Chirac was also hit by a wave of public sector strikes when he attempted to impose strict limits on wage increases as part of a broader deflationary policy. Mitterrand was able to project himself as being above party and for national unity. His stock rose accordingly.

1982: Owen, 'libertarian tradition of decentralised socialism'

Having lost the election in 1979, Labour appeared poised for a quick comeback. Opinion polls gave Labour a 12.5 per cent lead over the Conservatives at the end of 1980. This was despite the fact that Labour had ignored public opinion and elected Michael Foot (aged 67) leader after Callaghan's resignation. Polls had shown that the former chancellor, Denis Healey, was more popular. Healey was elected deputy leader. The lead in the opinion polls was also surprising because Labour adopted unilateral nuclear disarmament, withdrawal from the EEC and a programme of extensive nationalisation. Labour had decided that in future its leader would be elected by an electoral college and not just by MPs. MPs, it could be argued, are more aware of how the leader performs in the Commons, and are more likely to consider the broader electorate's views. Against that there was a feeling that all parts of the Labour movement should have a say – those who do the menial party work and those who find the funds. It was decided that in future an electoral college would elect the leader, with MPs having 30 per cent of the vote, party members 30 per cent and affiliated trade unions 40 per cent.

Two factors badly damaged Labour's situation: first, the defection of the pro-EEC rebels and second, the Falklands War. Former cabinet ministers Roy Jenkins, David Owen, William Rogers and Shirley Williams issued their Limehouse Declaration in January 1981, and in March established the Social Democratic Party (SDP). Their declaration was middle of the road Labour: for multilateral disarmament, for NATO, for EC membership, for the UN, for the Commonwealth, for the mixed economy. They expressed the desire to join the Socialist International but were thwarted by Labour's opposition.[14] From the start there were sharp differences between Owen and Jenkins. Jenkins favoured a new centre party and was seeking an early merger with the Liberals. Owen wanted to turn away from 'Fabian paternalism' pursuing state Socialism in favour of the 'radical democratic libertarian tradition of decentralized socialism' identified with Robert Owen, William Morris and G.D.H. Cole 'and developing policies for individuals, families and small communities'.[15] He was in favour of an alliance with the Liberals, which was formed in the autumn of 1981. This alliance then won three spectacular by-election victories from the Conservatives. By January 1982 polls put the SDP–Liberal Alliance ahead of the other two parties, with the Conservatives trailing behind Labour. In June 1982 the SDP had thirty MPs, the Liberals eleven.[16] The world slump and Thatcher's policies had made the Conservatives very unpopular. The Alliance seemed to stand for co-operation, not confrontation. David Steel, the Liberal leader, and his SDP allies came across as civilised, sensible reformers. Steel and Owen also had the advantage of good looks and intelligence. In the Labour Party itself, Labour Solidarity, with such prominent members as Healey, Roy Hattersley and John Smith, fought a rearguard action against the Bennite Left.[17]

The other major event to hit Labour was the war, in April 1982, between Britain and Argentina which resulted from Argentina's invasion of the Falklands Islands, a British colony, in the South Atlantic. Thatcher took decisive action and a British taskforce of over 100 ships and 27,000 personnel embarked on a hazardous, yet brilliantly successful, mission to retake the islands. Of the British forces 255 were killed and 777 wounded; the Argentinians suffered considerably greater losses. Tony Benn and about thirty Labour MPs opposed the mission.[18] The majority of the public and of the two main parties agreed with the expedition. The Falklands triumph set the scene for Thatcher's second election victory. It came on 9 June 1983. Despite over 3 million unemployed, against 1.2 million when they took over, the Conservatives swept back. Luckily for Thatcher, rising North Sea oil revenues also boosted government revenues and helped to maintain welfare payments and the balance of external trade.

On a lower turnout of 72.7 per cent against 76 per cent in 1979, and with 1 per cent fewer votes, the Conservatives increased their majority from 43 to 144. Labour received only 28 per cent of the vote, its lowest proportion since 1918. The Alliance gained 26 per cent but most of the SDP MPs lost their seats, including Rogers and Williams. Benn was among Labour's casualties. Foot and Healey resigned as Labour's leader and deputy leader respectively, and Neil Kinnock and Roy Hattersley succeeded them.

Italy's PSI: An 'authoritarian-paternalistic Presidential party'?

As Labour crashed in Britain its ally in Italy, the PSI, was undergoing a renaissance. In the 1983 election it gained over 11 per cent of the vote, its best result since 1968. It was the largest of the smaller Italian parties and was in a pivotal position in the nation's coalition system. Its leader, Bettino Craxi, was elected head of government in a five-party coalition. He was only the second non-DC premier since 1944 and proved to have staying power. He served from August 1983 to April 1987. Of his many predecessors only two had served longer since 1945. Yet Craxi's success was the start of the decline of the PSI. His style of leadership has been characterised as 'authoritarian-paternalistic Presidential'.[19] This characterisation was partly due to Craxi's initial popularity with PSI functionaries, who felt he was doing a good job in restoring the party's fortunes. Second, the increased tendency of parties to project the leader in the mass media, which in turn reduces the importance of ordinary members and supporters, also played a part. The centralised structure of the PSI helped Craxi gain the upper hand against opposition within the party. Craxi shed any remaining Marxist heritage and strove to gain as much influence as possible. After nearly forty years in office the DC had lost much of its credibility, and hoped association with an apparently dynamic and modern force would help it. It joined forces with the PSI, the

PSDI, the Republicans and the Liberals, and put itself under Craxi's premiership. The improving economic conditions of the 1980s helped the DC and the PSI, both of which showed gains in the 1987 elections (to 34.3 and 14.3 per cent respectively). Feeling more confident, the DC took the premiership once again but the five-party-coalition continued into the 1990s. What had Craxi achieved? He managed to annul the system of automatic wage indexation, a product of the 1960s trade union struggle. This contributed to a lowering of inflation. He also renegotiated the 1929 Lateran accords between the Vatican and the Italian state, which had given the Roman Catholic Church so much influence. He was unable to reduce the increasing budget deficit and public sector debt. This was because too many DC, and more recently, PSI supporters benefited from this state spending. As the PSI party became more integrated into the ruling structures, so it behaved more like its earlier rival and current partner, the DC, enjoying the spoils of office. Its problem was that, unlike the DC, it had lost its traditional supporters and was dependent on floating voters who would desert it in bad times. It 'acted as a magnet for dubious financiers, bogus architects, pop intellectuals, the vulgar fringes of the new rich, place-seekers and time-servers'.[20] How had its other arch-rival, the PCI, fared in the 1980s?

To a degree the PCI was following the PSI down the path of integration into the Italian system, with all the dangers which that posed. The DC had taken its help in the 1970s without offering it office; in the 1980s the PSI was seen as an appropriate partner by the DC. The PCI continued to be embarrassed by its Soviet connection. It denounced the Soviet invasion of Afghanistan in 1979 and the crushing of Solidarity in Poland in 1981, but it still took money, directly and secretly, as well as through trading its publications, from the Soviet Union. And it found it impossible to conclude that the Soviet Union was a 'revolution betrayed'. The PCI was also traumatised by the sudden death, in 1984, of its leader Berlinguer, whose gaunt, intellectual features had given the party a certain dignity. His replacement, Alessandro Natta, failed to stop the party's decline. Its percentage vote fell from 30.4 in 1979 to 29.9 in 1983 and 26.6 in 1987. Natta then made way for Achille Occhetto. Occhetto wanted to go on reforming the PCI in the direction of Social Democracy, but without overtly breaking with its past. The collapse of the Communist regimes in 1989–90 forced it into a more thorough re-examination of itself.

1983: Kinnock fights those who 'treat realism as treachery'

Having taken stock, in 1983 the new leaders Kinnock and Hattersley started the process of revising Labour's policies, image and organisation by overcoming those who 'treat realism as treachery'.[21] Kinnock came under attack from the Conservatives and SDP and also from the Left in the Labour Party. He denounced the Militant Tendency, a Marxist group that had gained ascendancy in Labour constituencies, especially Liverpool. He also distanced himself from Arthur Scargill, the miners' leader who led his members into the disastrous strike of 1983–4. Thatcher scored by the sale of council houses and privatisations such as that of British Telecom. In 1987, '40 per cent of council house *owners* voted Conservative, virtually the same as the Tories' global share of the vote, only 25 per cent of council house *tenants* did'.[22] Kinnock fought a good campaign in 1987 but Thatcher scored her third successive victory. The Conservatives suffered a net loss of twenty-one seats and Labour a net gain of twenty. The Labour vote rose by 3.2 per cent and the party re-established itself as the main opposition to the Conservatives, but it lost seats to the Conservatives in London and the south. The truth was that most voters felt better off and were afraid of Labour as the high-tax party. The Alliance suffered by having two leaders – David Steel and David Owen – who seemed on occasion to be looking in different directions.

Having revised Labour's opposition to the EEC, Kinnock now abandoned unilateral nuclear disarmament but was forced to retract his abandonment.[23] His leadership reached its lowest ebb in 1988. By 9 May 1989, however, the Labour NEC voted by seventeen votes to eight to adopt a policy of multilateral disarmament.[24] It also voted to abandon nationalisation and recognised Britain's place in the EEC. Benn believed that on that day the NEC 'abandoned socialist aspirations ... and may be in a state of terminal decline'.[25] Labour was helped by other factors. It was boosted by winning the third direct elections to the European Parliament in June 1989. Turnout was only 35.9 per cent, of which Labour attracted 40.1 per cent, the Conservatives 34.7, the Liberal Democrats only 6.7 and the Greens an amazing 14.9. Labour had fought as the pro-Europe party, the Conservatives on an anti-EC platform. Another boost for Labour was the end of the SDP. In January 1988 the SDP and the Liberals agreed to merge. Owen refused to go along with this and attempted to re-form the SDP. After poor by-election results the committee of the SDP voted, on 3 June 1990, by seventeen to five to suspend the party constitution, thus terminating the SDP's activities. Many of their positions were later endorsed by Labour politicians who had bitterly opposed them when they were still in the Labour Party. The SDP had been divided from the start and was a victim of the British electoral system.

By the end of the 1980s the economy was in recession. Thatcher got into a muddle over Europe and was, in a sensational turn of events, replaced as Conservative leader in November 1990 by John Major, who briefly restored the popularity of his party. Like Kinnock, Major came from a humble background, but unlike Kinnock he had not had a university education. He initiated policies Labour might have been expected to pursue. He introduced a Citizen's Charter (which Labour-controlled York and Sheffield already had), enabled polytechnics to become universities, replaced the detested Thatcherite 'poll tax', raised child allowances and wanted Britain 'at the centre of Europe'. Major even called for a 'classless society', something Labour politicians rarely spoke about.

1982: Revival in Sweden

In 1976 the Swedish Social Democrats (SAP) lost power after forty-four years of continuous government. This dramatic change was brought about by a relatively small shift in votes (see Table 8.2 below). Over 90 per cent of the voters turned out to vote but it was not clear what they had voted for. One of the dominant issues in the election was the question of nuclear power. The SAP government of Olof Palme had committed Sweden to a large-scale expansion of nuclear power. This was on the basis that Sweden had large deposits of uranium but had to import 70 per cent of its fuel in the form of oil. The opposition was divided on the issue. The Centre Party opposed the nuclear option and the Liberals expressed strong reservations. The SAP's ally, the Left-Communists, also opposed nuclear power. Only the (Conservative) Moderate Party supported it. The SAP had ignored public opinion polls revealing that a majority of the electorate rejected any further expansion. A more specifically Socialist proposal came under attack during the election. This was the Meidner Plan for the creation, by a levy on profits, of workers' funds that would be used to buy a growing and ultimately dominant share of the equity in private firms. The SAP gave no pledge to implement this proposal, offering instead a commission to consider the whole question of workers' participation.

After the election Palme resigned and a non-Socialist coalition was formed under Torbjörn Fälldin of the Centre Party. The coalition collapsed no less than three times in six years and was defeated in 1982 when the Social Democrats were returned to office. Basically some voters had tired of the SAP and the changing social structure had made some reluctant to vote for a Socialist party; they preferred those who promised lower taxes. However, the non-Socialist coalition was not regarded as competent, and most voters did not want any tampering with Sweden's well-developed welfare system. The coalition partners attempted to demonstrate that they were not aiming at counter-revolution. They chose to maintain full employment by subsidies (the opposite of Thatcherism) and even nationalised the shipyards, steel and raw material industries.[26] They devalued the currency in 1976, 1977 and 1981. The non-Socialists were hit, like all office-holding parties in Europe, by the recession of the early 1980s. Sweden suffered more than many countries, as it was highly dependent on a few export-orientated sectors such as shipbuilding, motor vehicles and the extractive industries. The Social Democrats retained office until 1991, winning elections in 1985 and 1988. In 1988, for the first time since 1970, they won more seats than the three right-of-centre parties together.[27] The Communists achieved their best result for twenty years (5.9 per cent), helped, to a degree, by Gorbachev. The new Green Party (MP), influenced by the German Greens, attracted 5.5 per cent, which entitled it to twenty seats in parliament. But the SAP was victim of the international economic downturn in 1990–1. In 1991, on a lower turnout, the party suffered its worst electoral defeat, with its share of the vote falling to below 40 per cent for the first time since the 1930s. The Greens failed to attract enough support to be represented in parliament. The anti-tax New Democracy made a dramatic entry, securing 6.7 per cent and the Christian Democrats gained entry into parliament with 7 per cent. Clearly Swedish voters were becoming more volatile.

However, the great shock for the SAP and many Swedes was the loss of their leader Olof Palme to an assassin's bullet in the centre of Stockholm in 1986. Palme had succeeded Tage Erlander as prime minister in 1969 and had moved his party to the left. The Soviet KGB attempted to influence him during his first period in office, 1969–76, but gave up.[28] He had been an outspoken critic of the

Table 8.2   Percentage votes in Swedish elections 1973–91

Party	1973	1976	1979	1982	1985	1988	1991
SAP	43.6	42.9	43.2	45.6	44.7	43.9	37.6
Left-Communists	5.3	4.7	5.6	5.6	5.4	5.7	4.5
Centre	25.1	24.1	18.1	15.5	12.4	11.4	8.4
Moderates	14.8	15.6	20.3	23.6	21.3	17.9	21.9
Liberals	9.4	11.0	10.6	5.9	14.2	12.0	9.2
Greens						5.5	3.2
Christian Democrats						2.9	7.0
New Democracy							6.7

Source: *Keesing's Contemporary Archives*

Vietnam War and the international arms trade and of Franco. He supported the Sandinistas and the PLO and was 'one of the most vehement opponents of apartheid, and would accept no compromises'.[29] Clearly, he had many enemies as well as many friends. This caused speculation about a conspiracy to kill him. His murderer was never discovered.[30]

1983: Socialists hold on in Austria

In February 1983, the OECD published a report that revealed that Austria was experiencing the longest recession in the postwar period. It also mentioned that Austria's recent economic performance compared favourably with the situation in most other OECD countries. This did not impress some voters who were only concerned with the situation at home. The politicians were under fire anyway because there was a whiff of corruption circulating in Vienna. Minister of Finance Hans Androsch was under the spotlight because of allegations about his personal finances. He had resigned in 1981 but was still prominent in the SPÖ. Once again the SPÖ fought the election largely on the appeal of Kreisky. The ÖVP attacked the large public sector, extolling the virtues of private enterprise. Kreisky stated before the elections that he would only remain in office if the SPÖ retained its absolute majority. As it

Table 8.3   Percentage votes in Austrian elections 1979–90

Party	1979	1983	1986	1990
Socialists	51.0	47.8	43.1	42.8
People's Party	41.9	43.2	41.3	32.1
Freedom Party	6.1	5.0	9.7	16.6
Greens	–	1.9	4.8	4.8

failed to do so he resigned and Dr Fred Sinowatz, the former education minister, replaced him. The SPÖ found a coalition partner in
the FPÖ. This party had been founded in 1955 out of a mixture of
former Nazis, those who sought their support, and Liberals. It had
moved nearer to the centre since then, appearing as a third force.
This government remained in office until 1986 but it was increasingly troubled by differences between the coalition partners.

Some foreign observers were becoming worried about Austria.
Dr Kurt Waldheim, former UN Secretary General, was elected in
June 1986 as Austrian president by a direct vote. He was the first
president to be elected without the backing of the SPÖ. Waldheim
was accused of being involved in Nazi deportations of Jews when
he served as a wartime officer in the German Army. Separately, the
FPÖ appeared to be showing its true colours when on 13 September
1986 it elected Jörg Haider as leader. The election of the handsome
35-year-old Carinthian leader represented the victory of the pan-
Germanic, nationalist wing of the FPÖ over its more liberal
elements. Later that month the SPÖ announced the end of its coalition with the FPÖ. As the figures below (Table 8.3) reveal, more
voters found Haider's party to their liking when they voted on 23
November. The explosion at the nuclear power station at Chernobyl
in the previous April accounts for the leap in the Green vote. Under
Dr Franz Vranitzky, the 40-year-old banker and former finance
minister, the SPÖ embarked on a long marriage of convenience with
the Catholic, Conservative ÖVP.

1982: SPD defeats in Germany

As we saw in Chapter 6, Schmidt was ousted from office in
Germany in 1982. The FDP withdrew from their coalition with the
SPD and backed Helmut Kohl (CDU/CSU) for chancellor. In April
1982 the SPD congress had voted for higher taxes and greater state

intervention in the economy as a way out of the slump. The Left in the SPD also rejected the updating of NATO nuclear weapons on German soil. The Right in the FDP would not tolerate such initiatives and broke up the coalition. The FDP itself split three ways, with some well-known figures joining the SPD. Kohl was now set to remain in office, much against expectations, until 1998. Realising Kohl needed the FDP, Christian Democrats voted for it in 1983, so that it would not dip below 5 per cent and thus be excluded from the Bundestag. Schmidt withdrew from politics and his replacement as chancellor candidate was the moderate Dr Hans-Jochen Vogel, former minister of justice. The SPD lost votes to the CDU/CSU because of the economy and because some voters were uneasy about its defence policies. Kohl argued that West Germany had American troops on its soil but that it had free trade unions. Poland and the GDR had Soviet troops on their soil but no free trade unions. It must be remembered that Poland was under military rule at that time. The SPD also lost to the Greens, who now became a factor in German politics. The SPD found itself in a dilemma in the 1980s in that if it was too moderate it lost ground to the Greens, and if it was too left wing it lost voters to the CDU/CSU. At its congress in 1983 the SPD opposed intermediate-range missile deployments and, under Brandt as chairman, veered to the left, something easier to do in opposition than in government. The SPD had opened a dialogue with the East German SED and together they formed a Commission on Fundamental Values in 1982. Erhard Eppler, a leading figure on the Christian-pacifist wing of the SPD, led the SPD side. Its brief was to promote disarmament and common understanding. Even within the SPD some felt it was giving too much ground in its efforts to forge better relations. In 1987, fielding Johannes Rau, the popular prime minister of Germany's biggest state North-RhineWestphalia, and political friend of Eppler, as its chancellor candidate, the SPD went down to another defeat. Once again the Greens took votes from the SPD. They were given a boost by the accident at Chernobyl in April 1986. Despite the fact that the economy was improving and Kohl appeared a benign, sensible man, his party (CDU/CSU) lost votes to the FDP and the Greens in 1987. As the new decade approached Kohl was looking less secure.

It was difficult for the SPD to score against Kohl in inter-German relations, foreign and defence policy. East German leader Erich Honecker made the first visit by a GDR leader to West

Germany in 1987. West German loans were granted to the GDR in 1983 and 1984. Kohl went to Moscow in 1988. Soviet–US agreement in 1987 led to the withdrawal of intermediate nuclear weapons from Europe. Who could say that Kohl was not striving for peace and understanding? Brandt, in 1988, claimed that by continuing to hold on to the hope of reunification the government was perpetuating a 'living lie'.[31] The SPD and the Greens were being 'realists' in writing off the 'dangerous myth' of possible German reunification. However, it was Hans-Dietrich Genscher, FDP leader, vice-chancellor and foreign minister, who was making the running in East–West relations, to some extent against the opposition of the more conservative forces in the CDU/CSU. Opinion polls revealed that he was the most popular German politician. One other problem hurting Kohl but not helping the SPD either was the relative success of the new Far-Right party, the REP or Republicans. This party claimed not to be pro-Nazi but pro-German; it stood for German unity and against further moves towards integration in the EC.[32] It also shouted loudest on law and order. The key plank of its electoral programme was opposition to foreigners settling in Germany. This was on both economic and cultural grounds. In the European elections of 1989 the REP startled everyone by gaining entry to the European Parliament with a 7.1 per cent vote. West Germany was taking in more refugees than any other European state. It also had to cope with ethnic Germans who were allowed to leave the Soviet bloc and it was home to the millions of 'guest workers' who had gone to work in West Germany since the early 1960s. Kohl had to take account of the fears engendered by this influx among potential and actual CDU/CSU voters. The REP and the Greens also benefited from the exposure of scandals of one kind or another involving leading members of the CDU, FDP and

Table 8.4   Percentage votes in German elections 1983–7

Party	1983	1987
	turnout 89.1%	turnout 84.3%
CDU/CSU	48.8	44.3
SPD	38.2	37.4
FDP	7.0	9.1
Greens	5.6	8.3

the trade unions. This was the situation in 1989 before the dramatic events of the summer and autumn in the GDR were to alter the political landscape com-pletely.

1988: Mitterrand wins a second term

In 1988 Mitterrand was re-elected for a second term; he beat his nearest rival Chirac in the second ballot by attracting 54.02 per cent of the votes cast. He was the first president of the Fifth Republic to be re-elected in a direct election for a second term. Mitterrand had aimed his main thrust at the centre ground, calling for a 'united France'. In a decisive move, he appointed Michel Rocard, a moderate PS politician, prime minister. When Rocard failed to get a majority in the National Assembly Mitterrand dissolved parliament. Chirac gained his revenge on the FN, having abolished the PR voting system introduced by Mitterrand. It lost all but one of its thirty-three seats. At the other extreme, the PCF retained 27 of its 33 seats. The surprise was that the PS did not get a majority. This was attributed to apathy among its voters. Nevertheless, the PS was able to form a new left-centre government and PS-led governments remained in office until 1993. Premier from 1988 to 1991, Rocard introduced a guaranteed minimum income, moved to a more egalitarian method of financing social security, made a major investment in education and reformed the legal system.[33]

In 1989–90 came the dramatic turn of events in Germany leading to the restoration of German unity. Like many other European leaders, Mitterrand was at first reluctant to see what was happening and contemplate German unity. He visited Gorbachev and the GDR reform-Communist regime which 'appeared openly provocative'.[34] Once the die was cast, however, he wished the Germans well. Mitterrand worked on, alone and with Kohl, to strengthen the EC ties. He felt it was even more important than ever to cement Germany into the framework of the EC. The result was the Maastricht Treaty of December 1991, negotiated by the twelve EC members after hard bargaining. It established a European Union (EU) based on the EC, which would, in addition to economic competence, have a 'common foreign and security policy and a common interior and justice policy'. It aimed at a common currency in the future and agreed a Social Chapter (from which Britain opted out). Although it was not a constitutional necessity, Mitterrand carried through a referendum on the Maastricht Treaty in September 1992. His 'yes' campaign faced a formidable array of opponents including the PCF, the FN, the Greens and elements in the other parties. Four days before polling Britain and Italy were forced to withdraw from the ERM in humiliation. This could have turned French voters against Maastricht. As it was Mitterrand narrowly carried the day. On defence Mitterrand kept close to the Gaullist legacy (with the French independent nuclear deterrent as its centrepiece) and maintained close Franco-German co-operation. The PS and even the PCF had learned to accept this.

In May 1991 Mitterrand replaced Premier Rocard with Edith Cresson, France's first woman prime minister. It was hoped Cresson would give the PS new vigour in facing the 1993 elections. However, she rapidly became unpopular. She caused outrage among anti-racist organisations close to the PS by advocating the use of charter flights to return illegal immigrants and failed asylum seekers to their countries of origin.[35] She was forced to give way to her finance minister, Pierre Bérégovoy, on 2 April 1992. Bérégovoy held office for a mere eleven months before the electoral disaster which engulfed the PS in 1993. As finance minister and premier he pursued an orthodox policy of securing a strong franc irrespective of the immediate costs in unemployment. Bérégovoy could not implement his promise to cut unemployment, a major reason for the PS defeat. Bérégovoy himself faced accusations of impropriety in that he secured a large interest-free loan to buy his Paris apartment. He committed suicide in May 1993, only weeks after the PS defeat.[36] At the time many saw his defeat and death as symbolic of the road the PS had travelled over the 1980s. From humble origins, Bérégovoy had been on the left of the Socialist movement initially, but became an early convert to financial orthodoxy after 1981. Mitterrand left office in May 1995 and died of cancer in the following January.

1991: Kuwait, 'biggest fire the world has ever known'?

British Prime Minister John Major followed Thatcher's line of backing the USA on the Gulf War launched to force Iraq's Saddam Hussein out of Kuwait, which his forces had invaded and annexed in August 1990. Kinnock backed the war but once again Labour was not united. There was a thirty- to fifty-strong pacifist faction within the parliamentary party who opposed the war as a matter of principle.[37] Clare Short, Tony Banks and John Battle resigned from Labour's front bench on the issue. Elder statesman Denis Healey expressed his doubts. Tony Benn, whilst condemning the invasion, opposed force and urged the use of sanctions against Iraq instead. He wanted assurance that the government would not authorise offensive action without a special resolution by the UN. Black Labour MP Diane Abbott was doubtful about signing Benn's resolution because she thought the UN could be the instrument of oppression of the Third World by rich white countries. Dennis Skinner MP wanted the resolution to include something on the oil companies and their exploitation.[38] Benn was joined by Edward Heath, former Conservative prime minister, in seeking peace with Iraq. They did not succeed, nor did ex-German Chancellor Willy Brandt. Heath feared that if they were attacked the Iraqis would fire the Kuwait oil fields to produce 'the biggest fire the world has ever known'.[39] He was attacked for such remarks. The Iraqis did indeed fire the oil fields and it took over a year to put out the flames. Kinnock did not gain from his statesman-like attitude to the Gulf conflict. The main beneficiary was Major.

'Like Gorbachev, Kinnock ... made a historic contribution'

At the outset of the 1992 general election the polls showed Labour ahead.[40] But the polls proved misleading and Labour went down to its fourth defeat in a row. Labour improved its vote by 3.6 per cent, yet the Conservative vote had fallen by only 0.4. The Liberal Democrats' vote fell by 4.8 per cent. Labour's actual vote at 11.5 million was the same as in 1979 but the Conservatives, with 14.1 million, had gained more votes than any British party previously. Out-of-date constituency boundaries had helped Labour to reduce the Conservative majority to twenty-one. As polls revealed, Kinnock was a liability for Labour;[41] he and Hattersley resigned with good grace after the election. Healey praised Kinnock saying, 'Like Gorbachev, Kinnock was a man who made a historic contribution but didn't actually benefit personally from what he had achieved.'[42] It must remain an open question whether the history of the Labour Party would have been different had the SDP secessionists remained in the party.

Table 8.5   Percentage votes in British elections 1979–92

Party	1979	1983	1987	1992
	turnout 76%	turnout 72.7%	turnout 75.3%	turnout 77.7%
Labour	37.0	27.6	30.8	34.4
Conservative	43.9	42.4	25.4	41.9
Liberal Democrats*	13.8	25.4	22.6	17.8
SNP/PC	2.0	1.5	1.7	2.3

Note: * Liberals 1979, Alliance 1983 and 1987

Chapter 9

Gorbachev and the collapse of the Soviet Empire
1982–92

1984: Moscow in 'a dangerously leaderless condition'

When Brezhnev finally died in 1982 he was replaced by Yury Andropov, the son of a railway clerk, who had been chairman of the KGB since 1967. The appointment of the 68-year-old revealed how important the security apparatus had become. He was remembered as a key figure in the suppression of the Hungarian revolution. As general secretary he was known for his unsuccessful anti-drink campaign. Andropov was already a sick man and died of kidney failure in 1984. More remarkable still was the 'election' of Konstantin Chernenko, a sick 72-year-old of Siberian peasant stock, as Andropov's successor. He had spent his life in CPSU work and rose by holding on to Brezhnev's coat-tails. These aged bureaucrats personified the decline of Soviet dynamism. British Foreign Secretary Geoffrey Howe wondered just how the Soviet Union 'could possibly have been reduced to such a dangerously leaderless condition'.[1] Across the Atlantic Ocean they were faced by Ronald Reagan who, although 71, was very dynamic. In Europe they faced West Germany's conciliatory Helmut Kohl (aged 52), Britain's robust Margaret Thatcher (aged 57) and France's diplomatic François Mitterrand (aged 66).

Luckily for the Soviet Union Chernenko did not see his 74th birthday. Lucky again was the fact that Mikhail Gorbachev had been groomed as his successor. Gorbachev was just 54 when he emerged as general secretary of the CPSU on 11 March 1985. His illiterate Orthodox Christian mother and his Communist grandfather defined his childhood. Both his peasant grandfathers were arrested and imprisoned in Stalin's purges. His father, also a peasant, survived war service. After graduating in law from Moscow University, Gorbachev worked for the Komsomol and married Raisa, a philosophy graduate. Later he climbed the CPSU ladder. As a rising Communist official he was included on delegations to both Soviet bloc and Western states. He was shocked to find living standards so much higher in the West, and political debates so much more open than at home.[2] In 1978 Gorbachev moved to Moscow as CPSU secretary in charge of agriculture, potentially a Cinderella job. But he enjoyed the patronage of Andropov and was promoted to the Politburo in 1980. When Andropov was elected general secretary Gorbachev was put in charge of the entire economy. He burst onto the world stage, when he led a delegation to Britain in 1984. Prime Minister Thatcher found:

> his personality could not have been more different from the wooden ventriloquism of the average Soviet *apparatchik*. He smiled, laughed, used his hands for emphasis, modulated his voice, followed an argument through and was a sharp debater … I found myself liking him.[3]

Nearer home, Boris Yeltsin, later Russian president, agreed: 'He operated with amazing finesse.'[4] Yeltsin was then first secretary of the Moscow party organisation, and he was referring in part to the way in which Gorbachev quickly established his dominance by promoting his allies and removing his critics. Gorbachev replaced fourteen of the twenty-three heads of the departments of the key CSPU secretariats within his first year and thirty-nine of the 101 government ministers.[5]

With Gorbachev came two new Russian words for foreign journalists, academics and politicians to learn: *perestroika* (restructuring) and *glasnost* (freedom of expression). Gorbachev realised that there was something seriously wrong with the Soviet economy. At first he did not realise how serious. He hoped that by investing in modern equipment in certain key sectors, and by attempts to move from command to motivation and incentives, the workforce would be more productive. The economy did not produce enough and what it did produce was often not wanted. It was heavily distorted by the Soviet leaders' obsession with armaments and the space race. The most talented of the Soviet technical intelligentsia were put to work in these fields. The Soviet defence burden was approximately four times that of the USA.[6] Consumer industries were always neglected. In this area materials were in short supply and initiative was not called for. Gorbachev did not have a clear blueprint and undoubtedly reacted to pressure. He certainly did not wish to see the destruction of the Socialist dream – he hoped to realise it. Some thought he was beginning to do that when a Politburo resolution of 24 September 1987 permitted small shops to be run by individuals and co-operatives. This was not unusual in the other Soviet bloc states.

To realise his dreams Gorbachev attempted to reform the media and make their news reporting nearer to reality. He stopped the jamming of Western broadcasts, starting with those of the BBC in January 1987. The practice of jamming reveals the mentality of the Soviet leaders and their fears that those of their own people who had radios powerful enough to receive foreign stations could not be trusted to use this facility responsibly. Gorbachev sought to reclaim well-known dissidents for the Soviet system. He invited nuclear scientist Andrei Sakharov to return to Moscow from his place of exile, Gorky. Once Gorbachev realised the state of the economy, and that so much of it was devoted to armaments, he understood the importance of reaching agreement with NATO about arms reductions. One other incident brought home to him the desperate need for agreement over nuclear arms. This was the near catastrophe at the nuclear power station of Chernobyl in the Ukraine on 26 April 1986. In April 1988 the Soviet Union and the USA guaranteed agreements signed in Geneva ending the war in Afghanistan. Thus ended the costly Soviet involvement in that country.

At the nineteenth CPSU conference in June/July Gorbachev advocated a presidential system for the Soviet Union and a Congress of People's Deputies elected by contested elections. This dramatic break with the past took place on 26 March 1989. Elections were held to the Congress, a kind of electoral college from which the deputies to the Supreme Soviet, the Soviet parliament, were elected. Although 750 of the 2,250 seats were reserved for the CPSU and other Communist-dominated bodies, some genuine independent candidates were elected. Among them were Sakharov and Yeltsin, who by this time was himself something of a rebel and wanted to move more swiftly along the reform path than Gorbachev. Yeltsin eventually made it to the 542-member Supreme Soviet, which, unlike its predecessor, became a place of lively debate.[7] At last the Soviet Union appeared to be on the road to democracy.

1987: Reagan, 'Mr Gorbachev, tear down this wall!'

At the eleventh Congress of the SED in April 1986 Honecker appeared impregnable. He had pushed through changes in the composition of the Politburo, which meant that half its members had joined since Honecker had taken over in 1971. With an average age of over 64, they were individuals of limited experience. They greeted Gorbachev but did not even pay lip-service to self-criticism. Instead the SED announced its utopian plans to make the GDR a world leader in the 'key technologies', including computer-aided design and manufacturing, robotics, nuclear energy, laser technology and biotechnology. In its attempts to achieve these aims it readily sacrificed more traditional industries including the consumer sector. The fact was that the GDR, like its 'Socialist' neighbours, was in decline. It had relied on exporting a range of industrial, oil and agricultural products at bargain-basement prices to the West to import essential supplies. But increased competition from Asia had cut demand for these exports. The fall in oil prices had been another blow. Its defence and security expenditure was a further crippling burden. In the 1980s it was forced more than ever to seek loans from the West and encourage remittances from the millions of East Germans who lived in the West to their relatives in the GDR. Western television and radio and Western visitors, without consciously intending to, brought with them ideas, which gained currency in the GDR. The relative success of the Greens in West Germany captured the imagination of many young East Germans. The Greens appealed because they were not part of the Western establishment, were better educated, were often conscientious objectors to military service and did not flaunt BMWs or other expensive consumer goods. Such young people in East and West were concerned about the environment and opposed nuclear energy. Honecker went on about 'imperialist plots' against the GDR but he was glad to be seen with such 'enemies' as Helmut Schmidt (1981), Franz Josef Strauß (1983, 1987) and even Chancellor Kohl when he visited Bonn in 1987. He hoped that pictures of himself with such Western politicians would legitimise him in the eyes of his own people. In fact, the East German people were looking for greater freedom as a result of these visits.

One event many East Germans saw as they watched Western television was the visit to West Berlin in 1987 of President Ronald

Reagan. Looking towards the Berlin Wall, he called rhetorically to the absent Soviet leader Gorbachev, 'Come to this gate! Mr Gorbachev, open this gate! Mr Gorbachev, tear down this wall!'[8] No one thought that within less than two years the Wall would be open and redundant. The aged leaders of the SED had no intention of following Gorbachev. One line of argument they used was that they were *ahead* of Gorbachev in many areas. They had a private service sector of the kind Gorbachev had just legalised. Their economy was functioning and they had always retained more than one party. In a celebrated reply Kurt Hager, Politburo member responsible for ideology, asked his interviewer from the West German weekly *Stern* (10 April 1987), 'If your neighbour changed his wallpaper in his flat, would you feel obliged to do the same?' Hager and his colleagues deceived no one with such rhetoric.

1988: Hungary leads the way

Like the Soviet Union and the other Warsaw Pact states, Hungary was reaching economic breaking point by the late 1980s. It was heavily in debt and its economy in no way satisfied the aspirations of consumers. Unlike the Soviet Union it had experimented in the economy and had a small private sector. Western-style banking had been introduced in 1987 and Western-style taxation in 1988.[9] Foreign investors were encouraged, and this policy included, from 1989, full repatriation of profits. Inspired by developments in the Soviet Union, dissidents founded the Hungarian Democratic Forum (HDF) in September 1987. Other groups followed including the Alliance of Free Democrats (FIDESZ). To meet the new challenges, a special Communist Party conference in May 1988 replaced Kadar, only months away from death, as leader with Karoly Grosz. Grosz was very much in sympathy with Gorbachev's ideas. In January 1980 Grosz promised multi-party elections and a law legalising parties, trade unions and other bodies outside the control of the Communist Party. In October 1989 the Communists renamed their party the Hungarian Socialist Party. In November 1988 the Alliance of Free Democrats was established as a party. In the same month the traditional Smallholders Party was refounded and in January 1989 the Social Democrats. Elections were held in March 1990, which gave the HDF 25 per cent of the vote, thus putting it ahead of the other parties. By the second round in April the HDF had won a majority of seats and formed a government with the

Smallholders and the Christian Democratic People's Party. In parliament, the Free Democrats, the former Communists and FIDESZ formed the opposition. One problem the new government had, and this was common throughout Eastern Europe, was that the voters expected that by changing the political system they would get immediate economic benefits. Not only were these not forthcoming, but pain had to precede gain. Price increases and unemployment followed. As elsewhere, privatisation also proved controversial in that state assets were undersold and the few benefited at the expense of the many. According to a public opinion survey in November 1990, after only six months in office, the democratically elected government commanded less public confidence than the previous Communist one had.[10]

1989: Solidarity rejects 'socialist pluralism'

In Poland General Jaruzelski attempted to combine being a Polish patriot with being Moscow's man. As Gorbachev was now conducting the Warsaw Pact orchestra the general sought to 'normalise' the situation through overtures to Solidarity, which continued to exist underground. Like the rest of the Soviet bloc, Poland was heavily in debt and attempts at price increases and other reforms brought strikes in the spring and summer of 1988. Walesa overcame the radical wing of Solidarity, which opposed negotiations. Jaruzelski used the threat of resignation to persuade the Communist Party to agree to lifting the ban on Solidarity. Negotiations ended on 5 April 1989 with an agreement to rescind the bans on Solidarity and Rural Solidarity, and to hold elections in which 35 per cent of seats would be open to the opposition. On a turnout of 62.1 per cent, Solidarity won, in the first round, 92 of the 100 Senate seats and 160 of the 161 Sejm (parliament) seats available for contest. In the second round Solidarity gained roughly 65 per cent of the votes cast and 40 per cent of the total electorate. Given the advantages of the Communists, Solidarity could not have achieved this success without help from the Catholic Church. Walesa refused the offer to participate in a Communist-led coalition of 'socialist pluralism' and countered with the view that Solidarity should form a government itself. After much argument Jaruzelski, as president, invited Tadeuz Mazowiecki of Solidarity to form a government. Once it gained office Solidarity split, and Poland was subjected to short-lived governments and a fragmented parliament with over twenty parties. Under the new constitution of 1992 a 5 per cent threshold must be reached for representation in the Sejm. Six parties gained representation in elections held in September 1993. The Democratic Left Alliance (SLD, former Communists) gained 171 of the 460 seats, the Polish Peasants' Party (PSL) 132. These two parties formed a coalition government. They had to contend with Walesa, who in 1990 was elected president of Poland. One curiosity of the 1993 Sejm was that the German minority, not subject to the threshold, captured four seats.

Polish governments, whatever their political complexion, were faced with massive economic problems. These did not go away with the change of regime. Inflation and unemployment followed, which helps to explain why the former Communists were to go through a revival.

1989: Gorbachev, 'Life punishes those who come too late'

Dissident groups continued to grow in the GDR in the late 1980s. The Stasi infiltrated them, and arrested and imprisoned their members when it felt the time had come. When on 17 January 1988 dissidents attempted to join the annual commemorative demonstration for the murdered (in 1919) revolutionaries Karl Liebknecht and Rosa Luxemburg they were arrested. When others were arrested later that month protests followed in GDR churches, the only institution where a modicum of free speech was permitted. In Bonn all the parties in the Bundestag protested. In May 1989 the SED scored another own goal. It falsified the result of the single-list local elections. Although most voters obeyed the call of the SED to support the official candidates, as widely expected, a significant number rejected them. Foolishly the SED denied that this was the case. Protests followed and continued at regular intervals.

In the summer of 1989 GDR citizens on holiday in Hungary, Czechoslovakia and Poland sought asylum in the West German embassies in those countries. Others sought refuge in the West German mission in East Berlin. They wanted to abandon the GDR for life in West Germany. Increasing numbers of East Germans had sought to do this by legal means, mostly without success.[11] The Hungarians, who had started to dismantle the 'Iron Curtain' between Hungary and Austria in May, allowed several groups of East Germans to leave for Austria. On 11 September Hungarian

Foreign Minister Gyula Horn announced that Hungary would allow those East German tourists who wanted to cross the border to neutral Austria to do so. Tens of thousands took this option and then travelled from Vienna to West Germany.[12] Their actions, seen on television, persuaded others to follow. With Honecker reported sick, the SED leadership seemed paralysed. Moscow offered the GDR no help. To avoid further haemorrhage the GDR closed its frontier with Czechoslovakia on 3 October. The day before, the GDR had agreed to allow 14,000 of its citizens camping in West German embassies to go.[13] A riot took place (4 October) in Dresden, as 20,000 East Germans attempted to board slow-moving trains taking refugees from Prague to the West. Gorbachev visited the GDR to celebrate its fortieth anniversary on 7 October. All over the GDR demonstrations were held demanding reforms. In Berlin on 7 October an unofficial demonstration was broken up with force and many arrests were made. Gorbachev was greeted with posters: 'Gorbi help us'. He pointedly responded in the direction of the SED leadership: 'Life punishes those who come too late.'[14] Meanwhile attempts had been made to establish new parties, starting with New Forum on 19 September. On the same day the Synod of the Evangelical Federation of Churches called for pluralism in the media, multi-party democracy, freedom to travel, the right to demonstrate, and economic reform.[15]

With demonstrations now taking place daily, the 77-year-old Honecker was forced to resign after the unanimous vote of his colleagues on 17 October 1989. Egon Krenz, aged 52, succeeded him. The fact that Krenz had been seen as Honecker's crown prince was a disadvantage. Moreover, Krenz had been chairman of the election commission which had presided over the falsification of the local election in May. Worse still, Krenz made the mistake of taking on all Honecker's positions as head of the SED, the Defence Council and head of state. Krenz did however introduce a small measure of unilateral GDR disarmament and reopened the frontier to Czechoslovakia from 1 November, which prompted a renewed exodus. On 31 October the Politburo was confronted with an analysis revealing that the GDR was virtually bankrupt. For the GDR to begin to pay its way it would need an unacceptable fall in the standard of living of 25 to 30 per cent.[16] Gorbachev could offer no material help. An estimated 500,000 people attended a demonstration in East Berlin's main square, Alexanderplatz, on 4 November and called for free speech, the right of free assembly and so on.

Among the well-known personalities were writer Christa Wolf, Jen Reich of New Forum and Markus Wolf, who was until 1986 deputy minister for state security. The Politburo feared the demonstrators would force a way through the Wall.[17] Meanwhile, demonstrations continued in other towns and cities such as Dresden, Halle, Leipzig and Schwerin. Unrestricted travel was high on their agenda. Krenz had been discussing a new travel law since he took office but no one expected the events of 9 November. On that night came the sensational opening of the Berlin Wall and the other frontiers of the GDR. A tired Günter Schabowski, member of the Politburo responsible for media relations, gave a press conference which was broadcast live, a first for the GDR. In a rather confused reply to an Italian journalist he said that all East Germans would be able immediately to leave the GDR through any border post.[18] He meant those who wanted to migrate, not would-be tourists. His reply made no sense and many East Germans thought that he meant they needed only to show their identity cards, get them stamped and travel. Without higher orders, and afraid for their own safety, commanders at border crossings in Berlin simply gave in to the pressure from the awaiting crowds.[19] Many thousands crossed the frontier that very night. The police and frontier guards had to give up all attempts to control the crowds. The SED had hoped to stabilise the situation by this move – in fact, they had lost control. Through the increased migration and absenteeism the pressure on the economy and services increased.

A new government headed by reform Communist Hans Modrow was formed on 18 November. Less than two weeks later the Volkskammer deleted the 'leading role' of the SED from the constitution. On 3 December the Politburo was forced to resign. Honecker and twelve of his colleagues were expelled from the SED; later they were arrested. Krenz surrendered his posts as head of state and head of the Defence Council on 6 December. At a special conference on 8 December Gregor Gysi, a lawyer, was elected chairman, a new position, to lead the SED. Shortly afterwards the SED became the PDS – Party of Democratic Socialism. In some ways as significant as the opening of the Wall was the abolition, on 14 December, of the Office for National Security, which had only recently replaced the dreaded MfS. By that time the crowds on the streets of many towns were calling for German unity. They had been encouraged by Kohl's ten-point plan of 28 November, which referred to the development of 'confederational structures between the two German states'. No one realised how fast the pace would be.

All this had been achieved without violence by the East Germans and very little violence from the side of the SED regime. Why was this so? Watching television the East Germans had learned to protest from the West German Greens and anti-nuclear Christians. The SED leaders knew that without Soviet military help they could not hold their people in check. The GDR military feared for their own lives if they used force, as they knew they would ultimately lose. The SED and MfS had prepared to defend their regime against armed opponents. They were at a loss to know how to deal with unarmed peaceful demonstrators.

1990: Germany reunited

Free elections, the first in GDR history, took place on 18 March 1990. Some complained that there was too much interference from West Germany, but the elections could not have been fair without such 'interference'. The ex-SED PDS was the best-organised party, with a corps of functionaries fighting to keep their jobs. They had printing presses, offices and all the necessary means to fight a modern election. This was also true of the CDU. The recently formed SPD, on the other hand, even lacked telephones and type-writers in the early stages. It received help from the West German SPD. Worse placed was Alliance 90, which had no major West German sister party. The PDS even received a little help in the polling stations when the votes were counted, as opposition votes were sometimes declared invalid.[20] None of these factors stopped the Alliance for Germany gaining 47.9 per cent of the vote on a 93.4 per cent turnout. The Alliance, made up of the CDU, the new German Social Union (DSU) and the small DA, were most clearly identified with the promise of early unification of the GDR with West Germany. The SPD gained 21.8 per cent and the Liberal alliance BFD 5.3 per cent. All these parties stood for German unity, but the SPD had been let down by the remarks of Oskar Lafontaine, who stressed the costs and difficulties of restoring German unity. He sounded less than enthusiastic about it. The PDS attracted 16.3 per cent. This was a decent vote based on the support of the political, military, security, state, media and educational apparatuses and others who feared for their futures. The small civil rights groups in Alliance 90 had wanted a democratic GDR rather than a united nation. They were out of touch with public sentiment. Lothar de Maizière of the CDU formed a broad coalition government, including the SPD and BFD, to negotiate with Bonn on German unity.

On 1 July 1990 the two German states were formally joined in a monetary, economic and social union. The (West) German Mark was introduced into the GDR as sole legal tender. Industries in the GDR now faced full competition from West German products and goods imported into West Germany. They lost orders at home and from their customers in the East. As East European states freed their trade they switched from GDR products to American, West European and Asian imports. Unemployment rose rapidly in the GDR.

German unity could only have been achieved by agreement between Moscow, Bonn and the three Western Powers. For Kohl and his foreign minister, Genscher, the breakthrough came on their visit to Moscow on 10 to 11 February 1990. By then they had good relations with Gorbachev. Undoubtedly Gorbachev's visit to West Germany in June 1989 had made a great impression on him. *Der Spiegel* (5 June 1989) reported poll findings which revealed that 73 per cent of West Germans had a positive attitude to the Soviet Union. This compared with only 13 per cent in 1983. It also published a poll showing that Gorbachev was much more popular in West Germany than US President Bush, Mitterrand or Thatcher. Scenes of almost hysterical enthusiasm confronted the Soviet leader, the kind of reception he did not experience at home. He needed German help and the Germans were ready to oblige. He was clear that the SED regime was dead. In February 1990 Gorbachev agreed on the principle of German unity, leaving it to the Germans themselves to decide the timing and method. The Germans reassured him on the question of frontiers, economic aid and other matters but insisted on Germany remaining in NATO. Later that month (24 to 25 February) Kohl and Bush agreed on German unity. Germany was to remain in NATO; and the USA would continue to act as guarantor of stability in Europe. A number of other consultations were held on the basis of 'two plus four', meaning the foreign ministers of the four victor powers of 1945 and the foreign ministers of the two German states.

The Volkskammer voted on 23 August, with nearly three-quarters of the members voting in favour, for the entry of the GDR to the area of jurisdiction of the Basic Law (the West German constitution).

The Unity Treaty between the two states was signed on 21 August.
The treaty was then ratified by the two parliaments with only the
PDS, Alliance 90 and the Greens (in both states) voting against.
Finally, on 3 October 1990 German unity was finally restored. All
this was only possible because, as Gorbachev told President Bush at
the Malta Summit (December 1989), 'We don't consider you an
enemy any more.'[21]

1989: Prague's 'velvet revolution'

The Communists in Czechoslovakia had presided over the decline
of a once sophisticated and prosperous economy and society. The
emphasis for years had been on selling arms to the Third World,
including Iraq, and exporting Skoda vehicles – cheaply to the West
and expensively to its allies. Internally they had paid lip-service to
demands for autonomy by the Slovaks. In theory their state was
federal. Like the SED leaders, they thought they could ignore
Gorbachev's reforms. In 1987 Husak, who had headed the
Communist Party since 1968, was replaced by Milos Jakes. One
orthodox Communist had replaced another. In January 1989
demonstrations on the twentieth anniversary of dissident Jan
Palach's public self-immolation were brutally broken up by the riot
police. Famous dissident playwright and co-founder of Charter 77,
the human rights monitoring organisation, Vaclav Havel was among
the fourteen arrested and held for several months.[22] However, after
the fall of the Berlin Wall, events moved rapidly. On 19 November
Havel formed Civic Forum. In Slovakia the Public Against Violence
movement appeared. In the following week massive demonstrations
in Prague demanded the resignation of the Communist leaders and
the end of one-party rule. On 27 November a two-hour general
strike revealed to the Communist leadership that the workers too
opposed them. The entire leadership resigned. The new leadership
attempted to salvage what it could, but on 10 December the
Communists were forced to accept a government in which Civic
Forum and the other non-Communists formed the majority. The
new federal government announced that it would prepare democratic elections and begin the transformation of the command
economy into a market economy. In the Czech Republic and
Slovakia similar governments were set up. Alexander Dubcek was
brought out of retirement to serve as the chairman of the federal
assembly and Havel was elected its president on 29 December. On

New Year's Day Havel granted amnesty to over 16,000 political prisoners and the following day the secret police were officially disbanded.[23] In June 1990 Civic Forum and Public Against Violence won the elections and formed a federal government. The Communists won 13 per cent. The peaceful nature of these dramatic events led to them being dubbed the 'velvet revolution'.

The Czech Republic and Slovakia split from each other to form separate independent republics on 1 January 1993. The differences which were apparent when Czechoslovakia formed after the First World War remained. The Czech Republic was more modern, democratic and Western European orientated. Slovakia remained economically less sophisticated and its politics were more dominated by nationalism. Hostility to the Hungarian minority, 11 per cent of the population, and other minorities, had been a popular tradition. The EU denied Slovakia a credit of $246 million because of the undemocratic tendencies revealed by former Communist 'strong man' Vladimir Meciar, who has dominated its politics since independence.

Vaclav Klaus headed the Czech government from 1990 to 1996. He rose through Civic Forum and when that movement split he led the Civil Democratic Party. He was a strong supporter of capitalism and the market economy and pushed through privatisation. His management of the Czech economy was widely praised. However, the Czech Republic had advantages in that it was of great interest to foreign investors because it was a compact state with a well-educated workforce, a variety of traditional and modern industries, and excellent tourist potential.

There was no 'velvet revolution' in Romania. Ceausescu believed his massive security service, *Securitate*, as well as appeals to nationalism and isolation could save him from catching the Gorbachev disease. But the masses got the news via Voice of America, the BBC and other foreign radio broadcasts. They took the lead given them by their neighbours. Demonstrations in Timisoara, populated by many members of Romania's Hungarian minority, ended in bloodshed on 17 December 1989 after resistance to *Securitate* attempts to arrest the Hungarian Protestant pastor László Tökes. Security police opened fire in Bucharest on 21 December when crowds called to support the dictator started to boo him. This was broadcast live on television. Ceausescu had to escape in a helicopter the following day from the Communist HQ. The secret police attempted to hold the line and fighting went on for some days, but when the army sided with the demonstrators the game was up. Ceausescu and his wife were shown as little mercy as they had shown their victims. They were given a brief trial, which was later broadcast, and were then shot on Christmas day. As elsewhere in Eastern Europe the Communists enjoyed massive advantages where they were quick enough to read the signs and repackage themselves as reformers, nationalists or Democratic Socialists. They had monopolised administration, business, the media and the police, and had all the necessary skills to retain their positions in most cases. They continued to enjoy finance from funds the Communist parties had hidden before their downfall. In any case, Romania, like the other Soviet bloc states, had little experience of democratic politics. By executing a quick about-turn the Communists succeeded in retaining power in Romania as the National Salvation Front led by Ion Illiescu, a former Communist secretary for agitation and propaganda. Illiescu and the Front won again in 1992 by a lesser margin. The Front was renamed the Social Democratic Party of Romania (PSDR) in July 1993. The PSDR formed a four-party coalition which included the Socialist Labour Party (SLP), also formed from ex-Communists. In elections in November 1996 the PSDR suffered considerable losses and Illiescu was defeated in the presidential election. Romania, it appeared, had broken with the reformist Communists who had assumed power in 1989.[24]

The position in Bulgaria was similar to that in Romania. Although, unlike the Romanians, the Bulgarians were pro-Russian, Communist Party boss Zhivkov had attempted to avoid a Gorbachev-style change. The day after the Berlin Wall was opened Zhivkov was forced out of office. He was later charged with gross embezzlement and sentenced to eight years jail in 1992. Like Ceausescu he had used nationalism to bolster his regime, turning on the ethnic Turks and gypsies. Petur Mladenov, successor to Zhivkov as Communist leader, changed the party name to Bulgarian Socialist Party (BSP) and led it to a narrow victory in June 1990. After widespread strikes, the Union of Democratic Forces (UDF) and the Movement for Rights and Freedom (MRF), mainly representing the Turkish minority, turned the BSP out of office. For several years near political chaos reigned. In 1994 the BSP was returned to office, winning 43.5 per cent of the vote (33.4 in 1991); the UDF attracted 24.2 per cent (34.3). Corruption and infiltration by the Russian mafia troubled Bulgaria. Economically it was hit by the war in Yugoslavia, when its main land communications through

Serbia were disrupted. Together with Albania and Romania, Bulgaria remained among the poorest countries in Europe.

1991: Gorbachev on the ropes

Few had expected that the collapse of the Soviet satellites in Eastern Europe would lead to the death of the Soviet Union itself. Yet this is what happened in 1990–1. On 12 February the Congress of People's Deputies amended the USSR constitution deleting Article 6, which gave the CPSU its leading role. Gorbachev had proposed that the Communists should accept this on 5 February and that they should work for a 'humane, democratic socialism' in a multi-party state. In a highly symbolic move Leningraders voted on 6 September 1990 to restore the original name of the city, St Petersburg. On 31 March 1991 the Warsaw Pact was formally dissolved. It is difficult to convey the sense of surprise, joy, horror and fear that these moves brought to various groups all over Europe. For old Communists their world was disappearing little by little before their very eyes. After about forty-five years of Cold War their old Western adversaries could hardly believe that this peaceful revolution was taking place. There was much more to come. Both as CPSU leader and Soviet president Gorbachev saw his powers dwindle over 1990–1. As the CPSU lost its power so its leader lost his political significance. Yeltsin, on the other hand, built up his position as chairman of the Supreme Soviet of the Russian Republic by strengthening the Republic vis-à-vis the Soviet Union. In June 1991 he won the first free election to the presidency of the Russian Republic, receiving 57.3 per cent of the vote on a turnout of 74 per cent. His declared aim, like Gorbachev's, was to transform the Russian economy into a market economy.

Despite the cracking pace of change the world looked on bothered and bewildered when a coup on 19 August was intended to overthrow Gorbachev. Led by Vladimir Kryuchkov, chairman of the KGB since 1988 and Politburo member, the plotters were men who had been promoted by Gorbachev.[25] They thought he had betrayed the Communist cause. They demanded that all institutions obey them and they declared a state of emergency for six months. In an act of courage and defiance Yeltsin declared the moves illegal. The coup collapsed because of lack of popular and military support and its leaders were arrested. Yeltsin then took charge of all Soviet armed forces within Russia and banned the activities of the

CPSU in the Russian Republic. One by one the Baltic states and then the other republics declared themselves sovereign and later independent of the Soviet Union. Eventually, without the three Baltic states – Estonia, Latvia and Lithuania – and Georgia, the remaining Soviet states established a new Commonwealth of Independent States in December 1991. By the end of the month the Soviet Union had ceased to exist in international law and Gorbachev was out of a job.

Chapter 10

Resurgence of Social Democracy in Western Europe

In the early 1990s some well-known actors – Gorbachev, Mitterrand, Reagan, Thatcher – disappeared from the political stage, and the public had to get used to new faces. Politicians seemed to be becoming less important as 'market forces' were enshrined on gleaming altars everywhere. Among the important new names were those of a number of tycoons, often in the media or finance. Deregulation of the media and privatisation of public industries gave these individuals a golden opportunity to extend their empires. Leo Kirch, the Munich media entrepreneur, grew in importance in Germany. In Italy Silvio Berlusconi was not content to wield indirect influence but went into politics. This was also true of Sir James Goldsmith, the financier, and Lord Rothermere, the newspaper owner, in Britain. CNN owner Ted Turner and News International's Rupert Murdoch were content to influence the world through their media empires. Bill Gates, perhaps the world's richest man, became increasingly familiar as the head of Microsoft, the IT colossus. A word or two from US financier George Soros and currencies could collapse.

Most politicians looked puny in comparison with such individuals. This was not true of Bill Clinton who was inaugurated as forty-second US president in January 1993. Calling himself a 'New Democrat', he had beaten incumbent Republican George Bush and Texan billionaire Ross Perot (independent). He was re-elected for a second term in 1996. Though liberal on social issues such as abortion, Clinton had made his way through tough welfare policies which appealed to conservative voters. Clinton found he had inherited several crises abroad – in Somalia, Bosnia, the Middle East and other areas – and the biggest federal deficit in history at home. It was questionable whether the post-Cold War world was any less dangerous than it had been during the 1980s. However, the former governor of Arkansas 'saw his primary goal as President to make the world safe for U.S. business and its global system of capital accumulation'.[1]

Clinton's victories gave some hope to Europe's Social Democratic parties. By September 1998 these parties had triumphed in Britain, France and Germany, and headed coalitions in Austria, Sweden and most other Western European states. They had been narrowly defeated in Spain and gone into opposition in Norway. What were the aims of these Social Democratic movements and what had they achieved by the end of the century? In some ways Tony Blair in Britain sounded the most ambitious and he followed closely the strategy and tactics of Clinton. Before Blair, however, there was the brief interregnum of John Smith.

1995: Blair, 'enterprise of the market'

John Smith was immediately more impressive than Neil Kinnock, whom he replaced as Labour leader in 1992. Smith, a 54-year-old Scottish lawyer, had the benefit of having held office under Callaghan. He was moderate, pro-EEC, and sounded middle-of-the-road Labour. Even more than Kinnock he went out to convince the City that Labour was 'reliable'. His deputy was Margaret Beckett, a woman long associated with left-wing positions. Smith continued Kinnock's work of modernising Labour and broadening its appeal. Although he had been elected with strong union support, Smith further reduced the influence of the unions on Labour politics. The 1993 party conference narrowly agreed a version of one member one vote, which eroded the unions' block vote at the annual conference and effectively broke the power of the unions in the Labour Party.[2] Under Smith Labour enjoyed a large lead in the opinion polls and made great advances in the 1994 local government and European parliament elections, capturing sixty-two (forty-five in 1989) of Britain's eighty-four seats to the Conservatives' eighteen (thirty-two in 1989).

Smith died suddenly on 12 May 1994. Tony Blair (aged 41) was elected as his successor, defeating Margaret Beckett and John Prescott with a convincing majority. Prescott took over as his deputy. Apart from having been born in the same month, Blair and Prescott appeared to have little in common. Blair's father was a Conservative lawyer and university lecturer and Blair was sent to public school and Oxford University. He became a barrister special-ising in trade union work. 'Closeness to the party leader turned out to be his passport upwards, not just under Foot, but under Kinnock and Smith too.'[3] He had opposed the EC, supported public owner-ship and joined CND and then changed his views when the leadership did so.[4] By the time he became leader Blair had altered his ideological passport in many details. Prescott (aged 56) left school at 15 and trained as a chef before serving in the merchant navy. After studying at Ruskin College and Hull University he entered the Commons in 1970. He had been well known as a leftist. He too had moved ideologically during the 1990s.

Blair adopted much from the Clinton Democrats. Labour was no longer the high-tax, high-spending party. It presented itself as the party of law and order, family values, and enterprise. In other words, like the 'New' Democrats it attempted to usurp the core values traditionally associated with the Right. It displayed a tougher profile on defence issues. It became New Labour. As a sign of his commitment to change, Blair gave the scrapping of Clause 4 of Labour's (1918) constitution top priority. He was rebuffed when he surprised the 1994 conference by announcing this move. The conference voted to retain it. On 10 January 1995, a majority of Labour's Euro-MPs sponsored an advertisement in the *Guardian* defending Clause 4, saying it could be added to but not replaced. However, a special conference on 29 April 1995 approved the new clause by a 65 per cent vote.[5] The relevant Clause 2 of the new 'Aims and Values of the Labour Party' states the party works for:

> A dynamic economy, serving the public interest, in which the enterprise of the market and the rigour of competition are joined with the forces of partnership and co-operation to produce the wealth the nation needs and the opportunity for all to work and prosper, with a thriving private sector and high quality public services, where those undertakings essential to the common good are either owned by the public or account-able to them.[6]

The new clause could be regarded as less Socialist than the Gang of Four's Limehouse Declaration (see Chapter 8). Whilst it does not exclude the possibility of certain undertakings being publicly owned it does represent a fundamental shift in policy. Labour had fully embraced market capitalism. Lord Rothermere, the media tycoon, believed this, and later supported Blair and his party in government.[7]

Gordon Brown, shadow chancellor and a close friend and ally of Blair, played a key role in the new strategy. On 18 May 1995 he gave an undertaking that Labour would not increase public borrowing. Later he committed Labour to the Conservatives' spending plans for the first two years of a Labour government.

1997: Blair's New Labour landslide

In the election campaign of 1997 Labour faced not only the Conservatives and Liberal Democrats, but the resurgent Scottish National Party (SNP) and the Welsh nationalists (Plaid Cymru: PC), both on the Left. On 1 May 1996 Arthur Scargill, the National Union of Miners' leader, broke away from Labour to establish the Socialist Labour Party. It fielded fifty-four candidates. The Scottish Socialist League put up sixteen candidates. The UK Independence Party and the Liberals (who opposed the Liberal Democrats) all made left-of-centre noises. Even though the opinion polls put Labour well ahead there was fear that something would go wrong at the last minute. As it was, there was a landslide to Labour. The party ended up with more seats than ever before. Labour won 418 seats (270 in 1992), the Conservatives 165 (336 in 1992), the Liberal Democrats 46 (20 in 1992), the SNP 6 (3 in 1992), and the PC 4 (4 in 1992). In terms of seats, the Conservatives were wiped out of Scotland and Wales. Labour gained in all parts of the country and for the first time outscored the Conservatives among the middle class and among homeowners.[8] Unusually, Labour won more Conservative defectors than the Liberal Democrats.

For Labour there were disappointing aspects to its victory. Turnout (71.2 per cent) was the lowest in the postwar period. As in 1992, turnout was much lower in traditional Labour areas than in strong Conservative ones. In absolute terms, Labour had only once before gained a higher vote – in 1951, when it was defeated in terms of seats. It gained a higher share of the vote in 1945, 1950, 1951, 1955, 1959, 1964 and 1966. Its vote in 1997 was actually smaller than that of the Conservatives in 1992. The size of Labour's majority was the result of the nature of the electoral system.[9] One problem for Labour was the question as to why its potential voters remained more apathetic than Conservative voters.

What was New Labour's parliamentary party in sociological terms? Never before had so few manual workers – 13 per cent – been elected on the Labour side. When Labour last won an election in 1974, 28 per cent came from manual occupations. A few more ex-manual workers were to be found among the former union officials elected. Of course, many Labour MPs were from working-class homes. Trade union sponsorship of MPs was discontinued in 1995 and replaced by 'constituency plan agreements' between unions and selected local Labour parties.[10] This was likely to further reduce the manual working class in the Commons. More Labour MPs (66 per cent) than ever before were graduates. Labour was heavily weighted towards public sector professions, especially teaching and local government. In absolute terms Labour's top professions were school teachers (fifty-four), politicians or political organisers (forty), polytechnic or college lecturers (thirty-five), civil servants/local government officials (thirty), publishers or journalists (twenty-nine), barristers or solicitors (twenty-nine), and university lecturers (twenty-two). Out of 418 Labour MPs, 111 were in education. Altogether thirty-seven Labour MPs (9 per cent) claimed business or managerial experience.[11]

Blair constructed his cabinet almost entirely on the basis of the shadow cabinet. Prescott was appointed deputy prime minister, Brown took over as chancellor, Robin Cook was given the Foreign Office, Jack Straw the Home Office and Margaret Beckett the Board of Trade. Of his twenty-one cabinet members most, including all of the above, had made their way by endorsing left-wing policies at variance with what they had now accepted.

1997: Jospin, France's future 'not xenophobia and racism'

Lionel Jospin took the PS into an unexpected victory in the elections to the French National Assembly held over two rounds on 25 May and 1 June 1997. It defeated the coalition of the neo-Gaullist Rally of the Republic (RPR) and the Union for French Democracy (UDF). Both parties were stunned by the size of their losses. The right-of-centre defeat was worst for President Jacques Chirac (RPR) who had made the early election a vote of confidence in himself. The total Left vote was 45.4 per cent, of which the PS claimed 23.4 per cent. In addition, the Radical Socialist Party (PRS, Liberals) gained 1.4 per cent. Particularly worrying was the Far

Right National Front (FN) vote of 14.9 per cent, which made it roughly as big as each of the two right-of-centre parties. The FN campaigned on a strongly anti-immigrant and Eurosceptic platform. Jospin cobbled together a coalition of PS, PCF, Greens, PRS and the Eurosceptic Citizens' Movement (MDC). His fourteen-member government included five women.

What was Jospin trying to achieve? He pledged an increase in the minimum wage. But like Blair's move on this issue, the planned increase was not enough for the trade unions. Again like Blair, Jospin emphasised job creation for the young unemployed, pointing out, however, that because of the serious state of government finances he would have to act cautiously. He promised a fairer tax system, which would include gender equality. He also promised the closure of the Phoenix nuclear fast-breeder reactor. Declaring that the future could 'not be built on xenophobia and racism', he announced a total review of immigration legislation and confirmed plans to grant residence papers to up to 40,000 (mainly African) immigrants and to restore the automatic right of citizenship to anyone born in France. Jospin sounded a more sceptical line on EMU.[12]

Table 10.1 Percentage votes in elections to French National Assembly May 1997

Party	Percentage of vote	Seats
PS	23.4	241
RPR	15.7	134
FN	14.9	1
UDF	14.2	108
PCF	9.9	38
Greens	6.8	7
Other Right	6.6	14
Other Left	2.8	21
Far Left	2.5	–
Radicals (PRS)	1.4	12
Spoiled papers	0.3	–

1998: Austria, no 'social dumping'

To some surprise Austria voted on 17 June 1994 to accept the negotiated terms for its entry into the EU. Only the small Liberal Forum
had been unequivocally in favour of entry. In the past some in the
SPÖ had feared the loss of Austria's neutrality. Farmers supporting
the ÖVP feared competition in agricultural produce, the Greens
feared environmental damage from increased traffic, and Jörg
Haider's FPÖ feared Islamic immigration. The two main parties,
SPÖ and ÖVP, campaigned for a 'Yes' vote, and of the 81.4 per cent
who voted 66.4 per cent voted for entry. Remarkably, voters in their
sixties were more enthusiastic than those under thirty, and men
somewhat more than women.[13] Among SPÖ supporters 73 per cent
voted 'Yes'.

Having accepted their chancellor's and vice chancellor's recom-
mendation on the fundamental issue of the EU, one might have
expected that the electorate would stand by the two main parties in
the 1994 parliamentary election. This did not happen. The trend of
increasing scepticism towards the two-party coalition of the SPÖ
and ÖVP (in government together since 1986) increased. More
Austrians came to feel that the leaders of the two main parties were
'stitching things up' for their own benefit. The opposition parties,
especially the FPÖ led by Haider, profited from this. There was also
fear of immigration as Austria was hit by waves of people escaping
from the upheavals in Eastern Europe, former Yugoslavia and elsewhere. The FPÖ continued to attract old Nazis and pan-German
nationalists. In the 1994 election campaign the SPÖ had once again
used the question of the chancellorship as the main issue: 'Es geht
um den Kanzler' ('The issue is who is chancellor') was its main
slogan. The SPÖ chancellor's wife gave a disastrous interview in
which she condemned mothers who went out to work to earn a bit
extra rather than staying at home and looking after their children.
She was roundly denounced by feminists and by the wider public,
especially as her husband, Chancellor Vranitzky, was a banker who
lacked working-class credentials.[14] Earlier, the SPÖ had received a
shock in the Chambers of Labour election. The Chambers are a
special feature of the Austrian system, designed to give blue- and
white-collar groups a direct input into legislation. The SPÖ usually
expected to get well over 60 per cent in these elections but only
attracted 54.5 per cent. Worse still, only 31 per cent of those eligible
bothered to vote, a new low. Licking their wounds after the disas-

trous election, the two main parties resolved to continue their coalition. The ÖVP, however, soon provoked a crisis over the proposed budget, which led to fresh elections in 1995. These gave greater comfort to the SPÖ than the ÖVP (see Table 10.2 below). Although it once again deployed the chancellor, this time the SPÖ concentrated more on policy. It sought to present itself as the defender of the welfare state and public services against neo-Thatcherite attacks by the ÖVP and the FPÖ. It agreed that reform might be needed but called for socially just reform.[15] With this appeal the SPÖ took votes from the FPÖ, Greens and Liberal Forum and mobilised previous non-voters. It gained most among women, pensioners and public sector employees.[16]

After having held office from 1989 to 1996 and thus becoming Europe's second longest serving leader, Vranitzky stood down and Viktor Klima was elected in his place. Klima had been finance minister and had presided over the limited privatisation of Austria's large public sector. As chancellor he attempted to reassure his own followers on the government's future course. He told a Social Democratic conference on fairness on 27 April 1998 that he would do everything to remove social injustices between blue-collar and white-collar workers. 'We are living through times when a neo-liberal *Zeitgeist* is trying to make us believe that we can only solve the workers' problems by lowering wages and cutting social benefits', Klima commented. He added that European Social Democracy had to counter these views so as to avoid a situation like that in the USA, where more money now has to be spent on prisons than on schools.[17] As regards equal rights for blue-collar and white-collar workers, there must be no 'social dumping'. The specific issues were periods of notice in employment contracts, provisions in case of illness and the pro-rating of special bonuses. This approach appeared

Table 10.2   Percentage votes in Austrian elections 1990–5

Party	1990	1994	1995
SPÖ	42.8	34.9	38.3
ÖVP	32.1	27.6	28.3
FPÖ	16.6	22.5	22.1
Greens	4.8	7.3	4.6
Liberal Forum	6.0	5.3	

to be quite different from the ideas of Thatcherism/Reaganism and to the left of Blair whose government continued to cut social benefits and continued the previous Conservative government's line on pensions.

1998: Sweden, upsurge of the Left Party

After suffering their worst electoral defeat in 1991, when their share of the vote fell below 40 per cent for the first time since the 1930s, the SAP bounced back in 1994 to take 45.3 per cent of the vote. The Left Party (former Communists) gained 6.2 per cent and the Greens 5 per cent. Against the SAP were the five right-of-centre parties, with a total of 41.2 per cent. The non-Socialist coalition cut unemployment benefits, imposed higher health care charges, and tightened the rules on sick leave. An internal market was introduced into the health service. The national debt increased as the number of unemployed climbed to levels previously unknown in Sweden. The result was the SAP victory in October 1994; Ingvar Carlson took over as prime minister. The outgoing SAP government of 1991 had applied for Sweden to join the EC. It recognised that Swedish business needed to be part of a larger market. The non-Socialist government continued the negotiations and in November 1994 52.2 per cent voted in favour of Sweden's membership of the EU. As early as March 1995 the Social Democratic government was in trouble and was forced to follow its predecessor by introducing more cuts in unemployment benefits and health care. It did however cut sales tax on groceries from 21 to 12 per cent and gave aid to the building industry and infrastructural projects.

The Swedish Social Democrats suffered a setback in the elections of September 1998. They lost seats mainly to the Left Party, which increased its total from 1994 to 43. Göran Persson's Social Democrats received their lowest level of support since 1918 gaining 131 seats (161 in 1994). Gudrun Schyman, a former social worker, leader of the Left Party, had campaigned strongly against Sweden joining the single currency and in favour of increased public spending. Her party attracted 12 per cent of the vote, up from 10 per cent in 1994. This was the best result for the Far Left since the Communist Party was formed in 1921. The Greens lost two seats, their number falling to sixteen. On the right, the Moderates remained with eighty-two seats, the Liberals fell from twenty-six to seventeen and the Centre Party fell from twenty-seven seats to eighteen. The Christian Democrats, however, increased their seats from fifteen to forty-two. They had campaigned on family values and as the anti-corruption party. Austere public spending cuts had cost the Social Democrats support. The Social Democrats had ruled Sweden for fifty-seven of the previous sixty-six years.[18]

In neighbouring Norway the SAP's brother party was also in difficulties. Norway was 'abnormal' in that its striking economic success did not redound to the support and re-election of the incumbent Labour (NDA) government in 1997. Since the last election in 1993 unemployment had gone down, inflation had fallen and growth had become strong.[19] With a population of only 4.3 million Norway was the second largest exporter of oil. The government had paid off the national debt and invested money to maintain the welfare state in the future when the North Sea would stop yielding its riches. The NDA was hit by the whiff of scandal, which marginally tipped the scales against it. After the general election of 1997 the NDA remained by far the biggest party with 35 per cent of the votes. However, the NDA lost 1.9 per cent of the vote compared with the previous election of 1993. Labour had ruled Norway for twenty-five years of the previous thirty-six as a single-party minority government.

After the Norwegian people rejected membership of the EU in the 1994 referendum (as in 1972) with a majority of 52.2 per cent against, Europe gradually disappeared as an issue. Norwegian politics began to normalise and frustration over being in opposition grew in the other parties. Labour policies were increasingly challenged in parliament. In the run-up to the election all the other parties tried to outbid Labour, either by calling for increased public spending or for tax cuts. When three centrist parties, including the Centre Party, declared their intention to form a government coalition after the election, the basis for the Labour government faded.

The NDA could look back on its many achievements. It had done much for women and the working class. It had also carried through the most important policy reforms for women: for example, the right to abortion, the adoption of an equal rights act, quotas for women in politics, more kindergartens, extended parental leave, equal pay for equal work and so on. Co-operation between the party and the trade union movement had led to a number of social reforms and had played an important role in shaping the Norwegian welfare state. These included the introduction of a Worker Protection and Working Environment Act, industrial democracy, working hours regulations covering all workers, sickness benefit guaranteeing 100 per cent compensation during sick leave, fifty-two weeks paid parental leave, and reforms of the education system which made secondary education available to everyone between 16 and 19 years of age. In recent years, an incomes policy, with a tripartite co-operation between the unions, employers and the Labour government (until October 1997), securing moderation in the annual collective bargaining, made an important contribution to the formidable recovery of the Norwegian economy. The incomes policy managed to accomplish a considerable reduction of unemployment, low inflation and low interest rates, an increase in real wages and expansion of public services.

As was the situation in many other countries, in Norway the Labour Party and the trade union movement had common historical roots. Over the decades the relationship between the party and the trade unions (LO) was adapted to a society in change. As traditional class antagonism lessened, the NDA saw the need to appeal to broader segments of society. Other unions that do not identify themselves with the labour movement or any other political group were challenging the Confederation of Trade Unions. Thus, in recent years, the NDA and the LO unions have developed a relationship that is more independent of one another. Yet there is still close co-operation between the two bodies. The relationship is built on consultation, the most important mechanism of which is a joint committee that is made up of the top leadership of the party and LO, which meets on a weekly basis. The committee discusses all matters of common interest but it does not make decisions. Until 1997 members of local trade unions could be affiliated collectively to the Labour Party. At its height, in 1952, the party had 91,500 collective members. This constituted a small minority of all LO members, but around half of party members. The last year before the system of collective membership was abolished (1996) the number had dropped to 20,000. Today the party only has individual members.

1998: Gerhard Schröder's SPD wins

Although in January 1998 the majority of Germans polled wanted a change of government, on the eve of polling Chancellor Kohl appeared to have closed the gap between his CDU/CSU and the

SPD. The September election, therefore, caused surprise at the extent of the SPD victory which ended sixteen years of CDU/CSU and FDP rule. Arguably, the SPD gained its best result in the history of postwar Germany. Only once before, in 1972, had it gained more votes than the CDU/CSU. But on that occasion the margin between it and the CDU/CSU was much smaller. The SPD had in 1969, 1972, 1976 and 1980 gained a higher proportion of the total vote, but in those elections there had been no left-wing alternative. As for the CDU/CSU, only in 1949 had they secured a lower percentage poll. At 82.3 per cent (79.01 per cent in 1994) the turnout was convincingly high. In only one of Germany's sixteen Länder did the SPD percentage fall – that was in Brandenburg (former East Germany), where some voters decided to help the Greens or the PDS back into the Bundestag. What had produced this result? Kohl had lost support, with only 39 per cent wishing him to continue, while 52 per cent wanted Schröder as chancellor.[20] Anger at the high level of unemployment (especially in former East Germany) was regarded by 85 per cent of voters as the biggest single issue.[21] However, the result could be interpreted as revealing that an absolute majority of Germans, 52.7 per cent, had voted for parties which had appealed for fairness, solidarity, help for refugees and the

Table 10.3 Percentage votes in German elections since reunification

Party	1998	1994	1990
In Bundestag			
SPD	40.9	36.4	33.5
CDU/CSU	35.2	41.5	43.8
Alliance 90/ Greens	6.7	7.3	5.1
FDP	6.2	6.9	11.0
PDS	5.1	4.4	2.4
Not in Bundestag			
Republicans	1.8	1.9	2.1
DVU	1.2		
Pro DM	0.9		
NPD	0.3		

Source: *Die Welt,* 29 September 1998

granting of German citizenship to foreigners living in Germany. That is not to say that most of those who had voted for the FDP and CDU/CSU had voted against all or some of these values. The three Far-Right parties – Republicans, DVU and NPD – the significance of which the foreign media always exaggerated, had been comprehensively thrashed.

What kind of voter had made the journey from CDU/CSU to SPD? The SPD had improved its support among workers in the former GDR but the CDU/CSU had also lost support among white-collar employees. In terms of age and sex, the biggest movement between the main contenders was among those over 45. This movement was particularly marked among women voters and, most surprisingly, among women voters over 60 who were more usually the greatest supporters of the CDU/CSU. This was true throughout Germany.[22]

1998: Belgium, 'cold, hateful, Machiavellian'

In 1995 the Belgian general election, the first under the country's federal constitution, returned the ruling coalition of Christian Socials, Flemish and Walloon Socialists. The combined Socialist vote was 24.5 per cent. The low-key campaign produced little change. Belgium was set to continue along the path of austerity to meet the criteria necessary for admission to the EU's economic and monetary union. The Christians were the main driving force behind this. The Socialists stressed their own role as guarantors of Belgium's generous social security system. They shrugged off investigations of some of their politicians for alleged corruption. However, they faced humiliation in December 1998, when Willy Claes, former Socialist Party joint president, former foreign minister, ex-NATO secretary general and deputy prime minister, 1979–81, was found guilty of corruption. Claes was just one of a clutch of senior Socialist Party officials convicted. Claes was forced to admit that Agusta, the Italian helicopter firm, and Dessault, the French arms firm, had given bribes to secure contracts to supply equipment to the Belgian Air Force. The money helped to fund their party. Although at the time there was no law against companies offering 'gifts' to political parties, the court found that the firms had been unjustly favoured in the bidding process. A second deputy prime minister convicted was Guy Spitaels, whom the prosecutor described as 'cold, hard, hateful, Machiavellian'.[23] Allegations about bribes had first emerged seven years earlier after the assassination of André Cools, a former deputy prime minister, 1969–73, and joint president of the Socialist Party, 1973–81. Cools was gunned down outside his lover's flat in Liège a few days after threatening publicly to denounce corruption. Another casualty was General Jacques Lefebre, former chief of staff of the Belgian Air Force, who killed himself during the investigation.[24]

The Belgian trial highlighted a number of problems currently facing Western democracies. One is the escalating cost of modern elections. Even in countries such as Germany where public money is available there is still the need to raise enormous sums. In Britain New Labour appeared close to having this problem as Blair's aides sought money from wealthy donors such as Bernie Ecclestone. Ecclestone, the head of Formula 1 motor racing, gave Labour a £1 million donation. Once in office, Blair exempted the sport from Labour's planned ban on tobacco sponsorship. Blair denied there was any connection between the two and the donation was refunded to Ecclestone. Labour also published a list of all those donors who had given more than £5,000. To say the least, tough laws are needed to control the raising and spending of such funds. The danger is that companies or individuals can come to dominate parties through donations. At the end of the twentieth century neither Social Democratic nor other parties had resolved this issue. Another problem highlighted by Belgium's travails is that of 'grand coalitions' of the main parties over long periods. Austria, Italy and Switzerland know this problem well. There is the danger that voters will become apathetic or turn to extremist parties if they perceive that the main party leaders are 'ganging up' on them.

Italy's turmoil

By the 1990s Italy's two main political movements, the Communists (PCI) and the Christian Democrats (DC), appeared to be cracking apart. The Communist tide had ebbed gently over the years since 1976 but in 1987 the PCI had still gathered 26.6 per cent of the vote. The collapse of the Soviet Empire led the majority of its members to decide it was time to make a fresh start. They followed the advice of the PCI Secretary, Achille Occhetto, and founded the Democratic Party of the Left (PDS) in 1991. This caused a split, and a breakaway group established the party of Communist Refoundation (RC). In 1991 the PDS garnered 16.1 per cent and its rival RC only 5.6. Italian Communism appeared in terminal decline. The DC also looked very sick. It still enjoyed the backing of the mighty Catholic Church, but the DC was embroiled in financial scandals. These engulfed such leading figures as former Prime Minister Giulio Andreotti. Moreover, as Communism appeared to be dying, some thought there was no longer any need to vote for the DC as the main bulwark against Moscow's Italian allies. Its vote fell from 34.3 per cent in 1987 to 29.7 per cent in 1992. This was its lowest ever vote. The Socialists (PSI) and Social Democrats (PSDI) also lost ground. Perhaps Italians were just getting bored and disillusioned with the old parties.

They were to get angry as well as bored, as increasing numbers of politicians were accused of taking bribes and kickbacks. By the summer of 1993 no less than 151 Italian parliamentarians were under investigation. This included 23 per cent of the DC, 34 per cent of the PSI, 47 per cent of the PSDI, 20 per cent of the Republicans and 18 per cent of the Liberals. Five PDS deputies (3 per cent) were also being investigated, as was one member of the RC and one from the Lega Nord.[25] This situation was to cause something of a political earthquake. Seeking governmental and regime stability, Italians voted to change the electoral system from one of proportional representation to one in which 75 per cent of the seats are elected by a first past the post system. The remaining 25 per cent are allocated by proportional representation. There is a 4 per cent threshold for parliamentary representation.

As Italy lumbered towards a new election in 1994 the formation of a new movement was announced – Forza Italia!. This relied on one man – the restless and charismatic self-made media entrepreneur Silvio Berlusconi. The name Forza Italia! (Let's Go Italy!) was actually a football chant. Berlusconi owned the football club AC Milan. He put forward an aggressive free enterprise programme. He wanted wide-ranging privatisation of welfare services, with citizens being issued with coupons to spend on heath and education at the institutions of their choice. He wanted to rid Italy of the 'parasitic-bureaucratic class' of civil servants.[26] Of course he promised massive tax cuts. A former partner of Craxi, he strongly attacked the Communists. He set up a National Association of Forza Italia! Clubs to help candidates locally. His candidates were young – 60 per cent were under the age of 50 – and 74 per cent had a university degree. Many of them were self-employed business people, managers or professionals. Berlusconi struck a deal with the separatist Lega Nord

in northern Italy, and with the ex-Fascist National Alliance (AN) in
the south. The result was the electoral victory of Berlusconi and his
allies in the March 1994 election, the results of which are given in
Table 10.4. Berlusconi was helped to victory by his ownership of
three of the six national television channels. His Forza Italia! gained
more votes from women than from men, and took votes from all the
old government parties. The Left parties had stood as the
Democratic Alliance. There was also a small Centre Alliance. A
government was formed with Berlusconi as prime minister. This
proved unstable and collapsed in December 1994. For one thing the
AN did not wish to lose the subsidies to its supporters in the south,
a measure strongly favoured by the Lega Nord. A non-party
government led by Lamberto Dini replaced Berlusconi.

Although parliament still had three years to run, President
Scalfaro called fresh elections in April 1996. A broad coalition of
Centre and Left which called itself the Olive Tree Alliance won 43.3

Table 10.4   Percentage votes in elections to Italian Chamber of
Deputies 1987–96

Party	1987	1992	1994	1996
PCI/PDS	26.6	16.1	20.3	21.1*
RC	–	5.6	6.0	8.6*
PSI	14.3	13.6	2.2	–
PSDI	3.0	2.7	0.5	–
Republicans	3.7	4.4	–	–
Greens	2.5	2.8	2.7	2.5*
Prodi List	–	–	–	6.8*
Dini List	–	–	–	4.3*
DC	34.3	29.7	–	–
PPI/CCD	–	–	11.1	5.8
Liberals	2.1	2.8	–	–
MSI/DN/AN	5.9	5.4	13.5	15.7
Forza Italia!	–	–	21.0	20.6
Lega Nord	–	8.7	8.1	10.1

Note: * Indicates member of the Olive Tree Alliance.

per cent of the vote; Berlusconi's alliance, the so-called 'Freedom Pole', gained 42.1 per cent (of which Forza Italia! secured 20.6 per cent). In addition, the Lega Nord secured 10.1 per cent, fighting separately. Of the 630 seats in the Chamber of Deputies, the Olive Tree Alliance captured 319, the Freedom Pole 246 and the Lega Nord 59. The Olive Tree's nominee, Professor Romano Prodi, was elected prime minister of a broad coalition. Prodi fell at the first fence when he miscalculated the votes needed to pass his budget. He was replaced in 1998 by Massimo D'Alema, leader of the PDS since the end of 1994. The former Communists appeared to be in a stronger position than ever before. However, this was on the basis of support for privatisation, greater European integration and the strengthening of NATO – all policies the old PCI had opposed and the RC still opposed.

Significantly, the PDS was not present at the meeting in Berlin of the 'European left parties' on 5 June 1998. Leading figures from twenty such parties attended, at the invitation of the German PDS. The most important parties represented were the French Communist Party and Italy's RC. They agreed to press for a 35-hour week in a bid to cut unemployment.[27] Could they eventually become a threat to Social Democracy by becoming genuine left-wing alternatives?

EU: 'Greater parliamentary democracy' wanted

What did the victory of the democratic Left in Europe in the 1990s mean? It certainly looked like being of advantage to women, partly because of the much higher numbers of women being elected to parliament and to ministerial office. There was emphasis on helping youth but it remained to be seen how this would work out in practice; the same was true for the lower income groups. Would the minimum wage policies be an advantage in practice for them? Would the Left's upsurge also mean a better deal for migrant minorities? Leftist instincts were to help political asylum seekers and the poor from other countries. But they had to square these generous instincts with the fears of voters that the influx of migrants was exacerbating social problems. There was also the issue that migrants sometimes brought their political and ethnic problems with them, with attendant violence and assassination: Turks against Turks, Kurds against Turks, Muslims against Hindus, Sunni Muslims against Shia Muslims, Serbs against Croats and Bosnians, and so on.[28] Linked with migration was the increasing problem of organised crime and terrorism. The organised smuggling of people over frontiers had evolved into a large-scale operation by the 1990s. Regime instability beyond the EU increased the likelihood of this. The EU placed its hopes on Europol, the European police authority founded in 1994. Its aims were to gather and evaluate data on traffic in illegal drugs, money laundering, car theft, smuggling of people and smuggling of nuclear materials. Some countries, Britain especially, had doubts about such an authority, and civil rights groups feared a European 'Big Brother'. The great majority, however, agreed with Austrian Interior Minister Karl Schlögl that, 'One state by itself cannot fight international crime.'[29] There were increasing worries about low birth rates in Europe and the greying of Europe.

Another area for decisive action was the future development of the EU. By 1998, the Democratic Socialist coalitions were pro-Europe, but they had to overcome the scepticism of many of their citizens and even of their own members. They were ready to carry on with the introduction of the single currency in 1999 (see below). They were agreed in principle on which states should be admitted to the EU in the next wave, but had a long way to go in agreeing on a redistribution of burdens within the Union. The Netherlands consistently paid more (net) per capita towards the budget than other members and was followed by Germany and, well behind them, Sweden. Fourth came Britain, a long way behind Sweden. At the other end, Ireland was the largest net receiver per capita, followed by Greece and Portugal.

Efforts to formulate a foreign policy dimension to the then EEC began as long ago as 1969 with the consultative procedure known as European Political Co-operation. However, only in the 1990s was there greater realisation of the urgency of formulating a common foreign policy. The fall of Communism, the Gulf War and the wars in the former Yugoslavia underlined this. A common foreign policy was enshrined in the Treaty on European Union (1992). The treaty was vague on security matters, and sharp differences remained between Germany and France, on the one hand, and Britain and Italy, on the other. The Germans and French favoured the building up of the Western European Union (WEU) as an autonomous defence body. The British and Italians wanted a European dimension anchored in NATO. These national differences did not change with the swing to the Left in 1997 and 1998. But it does appear that, although those states that are members of NATO will continue to support it, the WEU option is gaining ground. Meanwhile in Germany, the Greens moved to accept the use of German troops on peace-keeping missions outside Germany, something they had formerly opposed.[30] In the 1990s there was also discussion about the 'democracy deficit' in the EU. The Socialists formed the largest single group in the European parliament, holding 214 of the 626 seats in 1998. The Greens held 28 and the Far Left 33. In 1994 the then Socialist president of the parliament, Klaus Hänsch, wanted 'greater parliamentary democracy'. He emphasised:

> we are in no way trying to create a European superstate ... the diversity of Europe's peoples, cultures and traditions is not its weakness but its strength providing that we succeed in uniting our forces, exercising our individual sovereignties together and replacing the old antagonism with a new spirit of co-operation.[31]

Officially the European parliament became a co-decision-making body at the time of the fifth European parliamentary elections in 1999. Decision-making was shared with the Council of Ministers and the European Commission.

With Greens having gained office in France and Germany, environmental issues were being given a boost in those countries. Who could claim that this was not badly needed? To take one example, Britain's stored nuclear waste was a disaster waiting to happen, according to an official Nuclear Installations Inspectorate report in 1998.[32] Would the situation be much better in other nuclear-based power systems?

Social Democracy based 'on values, not on outdated ideology'?

Nowhere was the Left attempting to launch a frontal assault on capital, rather it was attempting to persuade the 'captains of industry' to be more socially responsible. Ideology was dead; Social Democracy was about values. As Blair put it, 'The essence of New Labour ... is the return of the Labour Party to being the great alliance of progress and justice, based on values, not on outdated ideology.'[33] The Labour and Social Democratic parties had long ago given up a Marxist-style 'expropriation of the expropriators' as their aim. They were trying to match their 'values' with those of electorates whose consciousness was formed by at least several influences: their social class, profession, status, age, sex, sexual preference, income, education, religious affiliation or lack of it, ethnic origins, their consumer preferences or life style and the increasingly fragmented, Americanised, mass media. One other factor which could be of key importance is whether they work in the public or in the private sector. Great differences existed in Europe in the mid-1990s (see Table 10.5).

The figures in Table 10.5 do not include those employed in charities and other non-profitmaking bodies, the numbers of which are considerable in some countries. These groups are traditionally more inclined to vote for Left parties than for parties on the Right. After growing over the 1970s, public sector employment had fallen in many cases over the 1990s. What would be the impact on left-wing politics if public sector employees perceived Labour/Social Democratic

Table 10.5   Public sector employment per 100 employed in 1994

Country	Employment
Sweden	33
Denmark	32
Norway	31
France	24
Finland	23
Austria	21
Belgium	19
Italy	18
Portugal	18
Ireland	17
Germany	16
UK	15
Spain	15
Netherlands	12
Switzerland	11
Greece	10

Source: OECD, *Das Parlament*, vol. 15, 22 January 1999

governments as less friendly to them than they had been traditionally?

By listing the influences which have helped to form the consciousness of voters it is easy to forget what the great majority of them have in common. Most share some kind of idea of social justice and a belief in the welfare state, particularly in health and education. Despite the prosperity of the years since the early 1950s, most of the electorates of Western Europe have in common their *lack* of property. The 1980s and 1990s saw the development of increasing insecurity. Deregulation of the labour market and recession saw to this. The advocates of 'market forces' wanted to follow the Conservatives in abolishing 'jobs for life'. Under their scheme of things everyone would have to go out into the market place to find 'clients'. Problem number one for the new left-wing governments of the EU was identified as unemployment. In the fifteen EU states about eighteen million people were registered as out of work in 1998.[34] The real figure was certainly higher. This was a figure equal to the combined populations of three member states – Belgium, Ireland and Denmark. On 16 March 1997 between 70,000 and 100,000 trade unionists demonstrated on the streets of Brussels, demanding EU action against unemployment. There were delegations from Germany, France and several other states.[35] Some were surprised by the demonstrations. They should not have been. Recent years have seen virtual self-mobilisation of masses of people in various parts of Europe – from the demands for freedom at the end of Communism, to the crowds in Britain at the time of the Diana tragedy and the paedophile backlash in Belgium in 1998. Most of the time, of course, the 'ordinary people' seek a quiet life to pursue their private pastimes, not to publicly challenge authority, let alone make revolutions. Someone said that in a revolutionary period millions of people learn more in a week than they do in a year of ordinary, somnolent life. That is even more true in the age of electronic media and increasing Internet communication.

Schröder, Jospin and their colleagues had to face the reality that the long-term tendency was for unemployment to increase, not decrease. However, at their Vienna meeting (December 1998) the EU leaders agreed on better co-ordination of economic policies to improve the employment situation.[36] The ability of the EU to eliminate unemployment would in part depend on the success of the new Euro.

Table 10.6   Percentage unemployment in EU states 1995–7

State	1994	1995	1996	1997
Austria	3.8	3.9	4.3	4.4
Belgium	10.0	9.9	9.7	9.2
Denmark	8.4	7.2	6.8	5.5
Finland	17.4	16.2	15.3	13.1
France	12.3	11.7	12.4	12.4
Germany	8.4	8.2	8.9	10.0
Greece	8.9	9.2	9.6	9.6
Ireland	14.3	12.3	11.6	10.1
Italy	11.4	11.9	12.0	12.1
Luxembourg	3.2	2.9	3.0	2.6
Netherlands	7.1	6.9	6.3	5.2
Portugal	7.0	7.3	7.3	6.8
Spain	24.1	22.9	22.2	20.8
Sweden	9.4	8.8	9.6	9.9
UK	9.6	8.7	8.2	7.0

Source: *Eurostat*, vol. 11 (1998: 57) and *OECD Economic Outlook* June, Paris (1998)

Growing inequality went hand in hand with growing unemployment. The 1996 *Human Development Report*, prepared by the UN, revealed that worldwide the rich were getting richer and the poor were getting poorer. The world's 358 billionaires had combined assets worth more than the combined incomes of countries representing nearly half – 45 per cent – of the earth's population. Three Americans – Bill Gates, Helen Walton and Warren Buffett – were richer than forty-eight nations. Yet the report showed that of seventeen industrialised nations, on the poverty index, the USA was bottom with 16.5 per cent of it people living in poverty. Britain was ranked fifteenth with 15 per cent and Ireland sixteenth with 15.2 per cent living in poverty. Sweden was in first position with less than 7 per cent living in poverty. Within the developed world Australia and Britain displayed growing economic injustice.

1999: Euro, 'power ... given up with so little fuss'

Undoubtedly, the most important innovation the new left-of-centre governments carried through was the introduction of the new single currency, the Euro, which began on 1 January 1999. This had been agreed at Maastricht in 1991, with Britain being granted an opt-out. It had started out as the brainchild of the EEC Committee on Monetary Union when it was chaired by Pierre Werner, 1970–1. Werner, a former prime minister of Luxembourg, who trained as a lawyer and worked in banking, was a Social Christian, not a Social Democrat. The project had been delayed by the oil crises of the 1970s. Eleven of the fifteen EU states joined immediately; only Britain, Denmark, Greece and Sweden remained outside. The expectation was that the coming of the Euro would boost inward investment and therefore employment in 'Euroland'. It was expected to lift trade by reducing the uncertainties caused by fluctuating exchange rates and by simplifying trade within the Euro zone. The British daily, *The Independent* (1 January 1999), commented:

> Rarely in the history of the world can power – real power, the power of money – have been given up with so little fuss. Eleven sovereign nations yesterday handed over control of their currencies to a committee of bankers. The meeting took less than 30 minutes.

Of course, the 'giving up' was the culmination of a long process of discussion and negotiation. It showed how far the peoples of Europe had gone in developing mutual trust. What about the committee of bankers? Bankers had often got things wrong in the twentieth century. Their dogmas had caused misery in the interwar period. They lost billions in bad debts worldwide in the 1980s and 1990s – money that could have been used on safer projects nearer home. As one critic claimed, 'No institution has claimed such prerogatives or has had such unlimited actual power since the best days of the medieval Catholic Church.'[37] Clearly there is a 'democratic deficit' here. But the critic admitted that national governments 'ultimately control all European institutions'. He simply did not believe they could act together. The Euro protagonists hoped it would give the participating states greater ability to withstand any turbulence in the international money markets, something which seems likely to continue, or even increase, in the twenty-first century.

'Unwarranted influence ... by the military-industrial complex'

General Dwight D. Eisenhower, Second World War Allied military commander, served as US president from 1953 to 1961. He was a Republican elected with the help of a variety of business interests. Yet in his farewell address to the American people he warned:

> the conjunction of an immense military establishment and a large arms industry ... new in American experience, exercised a total influence ... felt in every city, every state house, every office of the federal government. ... In the councils of Government we must guard against the acquisition of unwarranted influence, whether sought or unsought, by the military-industrial complex. The potential for the disastrous rise of misplaced power exists and will persist.[38]

Americans would have to learn to live with it under all subsequent presidents down to and including Clinton. Out of the top twenty arms companies in the early 1990s, fifteen were American. In the period 1990–4 the USA exported arms valued at $62,354 million, making it the top exporter in the field. Russia/USSR came in second with sales worth $21,912 million. The next eight in order were Germany ($10,536 million), the UK ($6,554 million), France ($6,287 million), China ($5,980 million), the Netherlands ($2,065 million), Italy ($1,997 million), the Czech Republic ($1,587 million) and Switzerland ($1,142 million).[39] This had not changed by 1997. Due to the end of the Cold War defence expenditures had been falling after hitting a peak in 1985. Gradually, new post-Cold War dangers were perceived in the Middle East, ex-Yugoslavia and elsewhere. But it was easy to manipulate defence expenditures to give sagging economies a boost. In 1998 President Clinton increased defence expenditure by 10 per cent to $280 billion (£165 billion).[40] This was the biggest peacetime build-up since 1985 under Reagan. The danger was that other states would come under pressure to do the same. They would need to sell more arms to help pay for their defence budgets. According to the Stockholm-based SIPRI, the value for deliveries of major conventional arms in 1997 was higher than the level recorded for 1996. US deliveries represented 43 per cent of the total.[41] What would happen to Social Democratic 'ethical' foreign policies under these circumstances?

Financial system 'close to ... meltdown'

> The need of a constantly expanding market for its products chases the bourgeoisie over the whole surface of the globe. It must nestle everywhere, settle everywhere, establish connexions everywhere. The bourgeoisie has through its exploitation of the world market given a cosmopolitan character to production and consumption in every country. ... All old-established national industries have been destroyed or are being daily destroyed.[42]

Replace the word 'bourgeoisie' with 'multi-nationals' and 'cosmopolitan' with 'global' and Marx's words of 1848 sound positively contemporary.

The Soviet system and its variants proved unable to create an economically viable and politically sound society, yet was not capitalism still unstable and crisis-ridden? Referring to events in 1997–8, George Soros told the British House of Commons Treasury Select Committee in December 1998, 'We came perilously close to a real meltdown of the international financial system.' The Hungarian-born billionaire cost Britain £7 billion, a staggering sum, by speculating against the pound in 1992. His actions forced Britain out of the Exchange Rate Mechanism, a preparatory stage of the Euro single currency.[43] Soros called for greater controls against speculators like himself to avoid the collapse of international capitalism. The crisis to which Soros was referring had started about two years earlier as a currency crisis in Thailand and had spread across Asia, going on to threaten the industrialised world. Henry Kissinger, the former US secretary of state, commented, 'No government and virtually no economists predicted the crisis, understood its extent or anticipated its staying power.' Kissinger attacked the IMF which, 'in the name of free-market orthodoxy', imposed inappropriate solutions usually 'leading to massive austerity ... I am disturbed by the tendency to treat the Asian crisis as another opportunity to acquire cheaply control of companies' assets and reconstitute them on the American model. This is courting a long-term disaster'.[44]

At the end of the twentieth century the world had changed in remarkable ways since the death of Bebel in 1913, of Blum in 1950, and even of Attlee in 1967. Mankind's scientific achievements were greater than most could have predicted and the wealth created immense. The great empires had fallen. The world hierarchy of states had greatly changed. Russia was perhaps *relatively* worse off than in 1900. Its empire was gone. Britain was *relatively* worse off. Its empire too had gone. The USA had moved to the centre of the stage. Japan, despite its lost war, had made remarkable progress to become the world's second economy. Germany's importance was even more remarkable considering it had lost two world wars. In 1900 China had lain prostrate before the world powers. Now it too was a top power. How would it use its growing strength? Brazil had become the world's eighth largest economy but it was a very troubled one. Others, for example India and Indonesia, were emerging. There were global corporations in the 'free market', responsible to no one but themselves, which were far stronger than many national states. 'Socialism' had virtually been and gone. Or was it nearer to the truth to say that it had never really been tried?

Castro's Cuba had managed to defy the USA for forty years, during ten of which it had stood alone. Loss of Soviet trade had resulted in a massive fall in economic activity. This forced some introduction of free market reforms. In 1993 Cubans were once again allowed to hold US dollars, and that currency became the effective currency of the country. Castro felt compelled to seek capitalist investment in Cuba, passing a law on foreign investment in 1995. Canadian, Mexican, Spanish and German firms were among the first to enter the market. Foreign tourism rivalled sugar as the main industry, and prostitution, drugs and widespread begging resurfaced.[45] Under Clinton the Americans tightened the blockade. This move was condemned by the European parliament and, in an extraordinary visit to Cuba in 1998, by Pope John Paul II[46] who called the blockade 'ethically unacceptable'.[47] The USA suffered a defeat in the UN shortly after, when it attacked Cuba over human rights abuses.[48] Some political prisoners were released as a result of the pontiff's visit. In the same year, Jean Chrétien became the first Canadian prime minister to visit Cuba. Since 1976 Canada had been Cuba's biggest financial partner.[49] In 1999 Chrétien criticised the imprisonment of four dissidents. Castro kept his grip on power as head of state, government, party and armed forces. He still claimed to be a Marxist. Whatever Americans thought of him, he would be remembered as a hero in South Africa and among many in Latin America.

Social Democracy had made a fantastic journey over the twentieth century. It had suffered some defeats, more disappointments and many successes. It could claim, more than any other political movement, to have brought political rights and social welfare to the masses of Western Europe. It had encouraged the women's struggle. It could claim to have done more than any other rival political movement to prevent permanent dictatorships of the Right or Left in Western Europe. Despite some lapses, it had helped colonial movements in their struggle for independence. Yet it was seen by significant numbers of voters as just another party of the establishment. It remains to be seen how much it has to offer the emerging nations and generations of the twenty-first century, whether it can adapt to their needs or whether another popular liberationist movement will replace it in the continuing struggle to overcome 'the Plutocracy' and lead us into 'the era of the Brotherhood of Man'.[50]

Notes

1 Before 1939

1 Marquand (1991: 41).
2 Steed (1985: 72–4).
3 Boyce (1972: 61–2).
4 Andics (1968: 64).
5 Maser (1990: 223).
6 Kerstein (1966: 78).
7 Kerstein (1966: 179).
8 Kerstein (1966: 191).
9 Beck (1982: 2, 208).
10 Beck (1982: 2: 207).
11 Bell (1967: 103).
12 Bell (1967: 103).
13 Krout (1973: 112).
14 Conrad et al. (1964: 89).
15 McLellan (1971: 221).
16 Marx and Engels (1967: 105).
17 Osterroth and Schuster (1978: 1, 83).
18 Berchtold (1967: 146).
19 Beck (1982: 2, 269).
20 Marx and Engels (1967: 71).
21 Osterroth and Schuster (1978: 149–50).
22 For the details, see Noland (1970).
23 Seebacher-Brandt (1988). *Bebel* is the main biography of Bebel.
24 See Marquand (1977) for MacDonald.
25 Kirk Willis, 'Russell, Bertrand', in F.M. Leventhal (ed.) *Twentieth-Century Britain An Encyclopedia*, New York/London (1995).
26 Beck (1982a: 1: 203).
27 Carsten (1982: 55).
28 Gilbert (1976: 457).
29 Galbraith (1977: 209).
30 Andics (1968: 210).
31 Weitz (1997: 299).
32 Kitchen (1980: 218).

33 Cross (1966: 319).
34 Cobban (1968: 139).
35 Cobban (1968: 145).
36 Sassoon (1996: 60–9) discusses these ideas.
37 Royal Danish Foreign Ministry, *Denmark*, Copenhagen (1956: 38).
38 Castles (1979: 25).
39 Castles (1979: 26).
40 Graham (1991) deals with the most important Spanish party.
41 Hugh Thomas' (1965) volume remains the most comprehensive account of the conflict in English.
42 Little (1985: 258).
43 Royle (1987), chap. 5, deals with propaganda in the Spanish war in the British context.
44 Buchanan (1997) covers all aspects of Britain's involvement. According to Buchanan, the ILP's contingent consisted of twenty men under Bob Edwards, later Labour MP.
45 Benson (1968) includes writers on both sides.
46 Read and Fisher (1988) gives a good account.

2   War and resistance: 1939–45

1 Jenkins (1948: 202).
2 Foot (1975: 79).
3 Brandt (1992: 109).
4 Brandt (1992: 109).
5 Branson (1985: 267).
6 Royal Danish Ministry of Foreign Affairs (1961: 93).
7 Seebacher-Brandt (1984: 224).
8 Seebacher-Brandt (1984: 234).
9 Sassoon (1996: 90), Jean Sagnes and Jules Maurin, *L'Herault dans la Guerre 1939/1945*, Béziers, pp. 18–19 and 43, show the confused state of the Left in the Herault.
10 Lacouture (1990: 347).
11 Cobban (1968: 190).
12 Mortimer (1984: 294–8).
13 Sassoon (1996: 88).
14 Thompson (1992: 71).
15 Ginsborg (1989: 13).
16 Ginsborg (1989: 55).

3   Social Democracy and West European recovery: 1945–58

1 The results are taken from *The Times House Of Commons 1950*, London (1950: 274).
2 Roger Eatwell, *The 1945–1951 Labour Governments*, London (1979: 116).
3 Hogg (1947: 113).

4 Author's long conversation with Attlee in 1963.
5 Ponting (1995: 742).
6 For a good account of the Greek situation, see Robert Frazier (1991).
7 For a good account of which, see Louis FitzGibbon (1971).
8 Churchill was speaking at Fulton, Missouri, when he used the term. It is believed that Goebbels first used it. For the Cold War, see Melvyn P. Lefflet and David S. Painter (eds) *Origins of the Cold War*, London (1994).
9 Brandt (1992: 137).
10 See Edinger (1965) and Scholz (1988).
11 Wallich (1955: 86–7).
12 Schwarz (1986: 689).
13 Pimlott (1986), 26 June 1952.
14 Avril (1989: 83).
15 Kavanagh (1998), Mollet entry by Peter Morris: 345.
16 Blondel and Godfrey (1968: 96).
17 Avril (1969: 258).
18 Blondel and Godfrey (1968: 96).
19 Blondel and Godfrey (1968: 97).
20 Ginsborg (1989: 85).
21 Ginsborg (1989: 116).
22 Seebacher-Brandt (1984) is one of the few biographies of the SPD leader.
23 Childs (1966: 40–1).
24 Sudoplatov (1994) is a fascinating eyewitness account.
25 Socialist Union (1956: 147).

4   The Stalinist model in Eastern Europe: 1945–61

1 This also happened in the Soviet Zone of Austria even though Austria was not classified as an enemy.
2 Furtak (1986), Naimark and Gibianski (1998) and Swain and Swain (1993) look at these developments.
3 Clissold (1966: 246–7).
4 Klugmann (1951: 116).
5 Klugmann (1951: 31).
6 Sudoplatov (1994: 335).
7 Knechtel and Fiedler (1992).
8 Pike (1992: 419).
9 Zauberman (1964) for details.
10 Sudoplatov (1994: 309).
11 Sudoplatov (1994: 328).
12 Andrew and Gordievsky (1990: 415).
13 Andrew and Gordievsky (1990: 410).
14 Mills (1982: 304).
15 Schapiro (1970: 558).
16 Wolf (1998: 76). Wolf was the head of the East German intelligence service.

17 Weber (1991: 49).
18 The details are taken from the *Manchester Guardian*, 'The Dethronement of Stalin. Full Text of the Khrushchev Speech', Manchester, June 1956.
19 Wolf (1998: 107) for SED's discussion of it.
20 Scammell (1986: 354).
21 Scammell (1986: 448).
22 Lomax (1976) for details.
23 Sudoplatov (1994: 367).
24 McCauley (1981: 181)
25 *Protokoll der Verhandlungen des V. Parteitages der Sozialistischen Einheitspartei Deutschlands*, vol. 1, Berlin (1959: 23, 68, 71).
26 *Protokoll* (1959: 27, 68).
27 Sudoplatov (1994: 201), Wolf (1998: 416–22).
28 Witnessed by the author on a visit to the Soviet Union in 1972.
29 Witnessed by John Howe and told to the author.
30 Gelb (1986: 70).
31 Bundesministerium für gesamtdeutsche Fragen (1969: 212).
32 Brandt (1992: 46).
33 Brandt (1992: 46).
34 Brandt (1992: 49).
35 Brandt (1992: 48).

5 Democratic Socialists, Communists and the New Left: 1956–68

1 Claudin (1978: 38).
2 Trond Gilberg, 'Communism in the Nordic Countries: Denmark, Norway, Sweden and Iceland', in Childs (1980: 230).
3 Seija Spring and D.W. Spring, 'The Finnish Communist Party: Two Parties in One', in Childs (1980: 176).
4 Blondel and Godfrey (1968: 92).
5 Sassoon (1996: 271).
6 In the *Nuovi Argomenti* interview in June 1956, as published in the British Communist journal, *World News*.
7 Sassoon (1996: 267).
8 Peter Shipley (1976: 219). Thompson (1992: 105, 112) puts losses at 7,000 in 1956 and 10,000 over two years.
9 Wright (1996: 54–6).
10 Hyde (1951: 271–2).
11 Darke (1952).
12 Thompson (1992: 101).
13 Hewison (1995: 107).
14 Thompson (1992: 117).
15 Thompson (1992: 121).
16 Foot (1975: 575).
17 Pincher (1986: 77–8) weighs the evidence.
18 Edgar Snow, *Red Star Over China*, New York.

19 Mackerras (1998) and Moise (1994) are among recent books examining twentieth-century China.
20 Grimm (1967: 46–7).
21 Winberg (1968: 382).
22 Marshall (1988: 43).
23 Marshall (1988: 55).
24 'Decision of the Central Committee of the Chinese Communist Party Concerning the Great Proletarian Cultural Revolution' (August 1966), as quoted in Winberg (1968: 425–38).
25 Shipman (1982: 1168).
26 Shipman (1982: 1194).
27 Parkinson (1977: 174).
28 Department of Defense (1985: 43).
29 Fraser (1988: 87).
30 Seale and McConville (1968: 22).
31 Fraser (1988: 129).
32 Fraser (1988: 205).
33 Fraser (1988: 214).
34 Seale and McConville (1968: 145).

6   The Climax of European Social Democracy? 1969–82

 1 Ziegler (1995: 157).
 2 Ziegler (1995: 183) quotes Peter Shore.
 3 Ziegler (1995: 91).
 4 Ziegler (1995: 5–6). The author watched Wilson on television.
 5 Ziegler (1995: 185).
 6 Ziegler (1995: 491).
 7 Ziegler (1995: 331).
 8 Ziegler (1995: 328).
 9 *Daily Telegraph*, 30 April 1999, obituary of Sir Lester Suffield.
10 Pimlott (1996: 432) claims it was not sudden, as Wilson had informed the Queen months in advance.
11 Ziegler (1995: 505).
12 Speaking in the Commons, 18 October 1973.
13 Thatcher (1995: 232).
14 Butler (1995: 29).
15 Henig (1997: 62).
16 Drower (1994: 29).
17 Winstone (1995: 147).
18 Marquand (1991: 174).
19 Marquand (1991: 174).
20 Bark and Gress (1993: 2, 157).
21 Bark and Gress (1993: 2, 141).
22 Wolf (1998: 250).
23 Ludz (1979: 203).
24 Bark and Gress (1993: 2, 257).

25 Bark and Gress (1993: 2, 247).
26 Sassoon (1996: 475).
27 Nugent and Lowe (1982: 254).
28 Sassoon (1996: 630).
29 Sassoon (1996: 597).
30 Sassoon (1996: 633).
31 Salmon (1995: 26).
32 Maravall (1982: 25).
33 Maravall (1982: 9). The author wells remembers his own surprise while visiting Spain in 1968 at the variety of political literature and the ease with which one could contact the political opposition.
34 Carrillo (1977: 146).
35 Carrillo (1977: 154).
36 Carrillo (1977: 164–5).
37 Carrillo (1977: 132)
38 Smith (1997: 462).
39 Nugent and Lowe (1982: 86–7).
40 Mintzel and Oberreuter (1990: 432).
41 Sully (1981: 51).
42 Sully (1981: 51).
43 Heywood (1995: 197).
44 Nugent and Lowe (1982: 87–8) for France; Mintzel and Oberreuter (1990: 151) for the SPD. Sully (1981: 52) for the SPÖ, Heywood (1995: 198) for Spain.
45 Sully (1981: 52).
46 Lovenduski (1986: 231).
47 Wilde (1994: 107).
48 Wheen (1985: 62).

7   The Soviet Empire: stagnation under Brezhnev, 1964–82

1 Schapiro (1970: 575).
 2 Scammell (1986: 449).
 3 Scammell (1986: 446).
 4 Robert Conquest, *Tyrants and Typewriters*, London (1989: 71).
 5 Brogan (1990: 224).
 6 Brogan (1990: 61).
 7 Brogan (1990: 63).
 8 Brogan (1990: 65).
 9 See Childs (1988) for details.
10 Childs and Popplewell (1996: 82).
11 Rudolf Bahro, *The Alternative in Eastern Europe*, London (1978: 244).

8   Democratic Socialism in retreat: 1982–92

1 Ambrose and Brinkley (1997: 321).
 2 Ambrose and Brinkley (1997: 321).

3 Ambrose and Brinkley (1997: 328).
4 Sassoon (1996: 639).
5 Sassoon (1996: 640).
6 Sassoon (1996: 640).
7 Cole (1997: 34).
8 Derbyshire (1986: 74).
9 Derbyshire (1986: 80).
10 Derbyshire (1986: 71).
11 Derbyshire (1986: 78), Cole (1997: 78).
12 Derbyshire (1986: 91).
13 Derbyshire (1986: 115–16).
14 Owen (1992: 497–8).
15 Owen (1992: 483).
16 Owen (1992: 512).
17 Jones (1995: 112).
18 Winstone (1995: 536).
19 Gundle in Gundle and Parker (1996: 91).
20 Gundle and Parker (1996: 95–6, 93).
21 Jones (1995: 114).
22 Drower (1994: 225–6).
23 Evans (1997: 27).
24 Drower (1994: 245–6).
25 Winstone (1995: 620).
26 Sassoon (1996: 483).
27 Sassoon (1996: 483).
28 Andrew and Gordievsky (1990: 572–3).
29 Brandt (1992: 395).
30 See http://www.fpsyn.com/servicesecrets.htm for the theory that Palme was killed for planning to close two NATO listening posts at Muskö and Karlskfona.
31 Bark and Gress (1992: 2, 532).
32 REP leader Schönhuber, interview in *Der Spiegel*, no. 6 (1989).
33 Cole (1997: 44).
34 Cole (1997: 154).
35 Cole (1997: 49).
36 Cole (1997: 52).
37 Drower (1994: 269).
38 Winstone (1995: 627).
39 Campbell (1993: 788).
40 Drower (1994: 299).
41 Drower (1994: 302).
42 Drower (1994: 328).

9 Gorbachev and the collapse of the Soviet Empire, 1982–92

1 Howe (1994: 357).
2 McCauley (1998: 30–1).

3 Margaret Thatcher, *The Downing Street Years*, London (1993: 461).
4 McCauley (1998: 52).
5 McCauley (1998: 54).
6 McCauley (1998: 66).
7 Westwood (1993: 508).
8 Bark and Gress (1992: 525), Ambrose and Brinkley (1997: 345).
9 Swain and Swain (1993: 200).
10 Swain and Swain (1993: 199).
11 Hertle (1996:54).
12 Hertle (1996: 69).
13 Hertle (1996: 74).
14 Hertle (1996: 81).
15 Hertle (1996: 77).
16 Hertle (1996: 92).
17 Hertle (1996: 104).
18 Hertle (1996: 146–8).
19 Hertle (1996: 166–77).
20 As witnessed by the author in Leipzig, where he watched the counting of votes.
21 Roberts (1999: 98).
22 Crampton (1997: 397).
23 Crampton (1997: 399).
24 Crampton (1997: 452).
25 McCauley (1998: 272–3).

10 Resurgence of Social Democracy in Western Europe

1 Ambrose and Brinkley (1997: 402).
2 Butler and Kavanagh (1997: 49).
3 Rentoul (1996: 85).
4 Rentoul (1996: 85).
5 Rentoul (1996: 420).
6 Rentoul (1996: 488).
7 In conversation with the author, 1997.
8 Butler and Kavanagh (1997: 250).
9 Butler and Kavanagh (1997: 316).
10 Butler and Kavanagh (1997: 206).
11 Butler and Kavanagh (1997: 205).
12 *Keesing's Contemporary Archives*, June 1997, 41694.
13 Luther (1995: 129).
14 Luther (1995: 131).
15 Fitzmaurice (1996: 295).
16 Fitzmaurice (1996: 293).
17 *News from Austria*, Federal Press Service, Vienna, 6 May 1998, no. 9: 3.
18 *Financial Times*, 22 September 1998.
19 Madeley (1998).
20 *Die Welt*, 29 September 1998. This was an analysis by the prestigious research body Forschungsgruppe Wahlen.

21 *Die Welt*, 29 September 1998.
22 *Die Welt*, 29 September 1998.
23 *Guardian*, 24 December 1998.
24 *Guardian*, 24 December 1998; *Daily Telegraph*, 24 December 1998.
25 Mark Donovan, in Gundle and Parker (1996: 105).
26 Patrick McCarthy, in Gundle and Parker (1996: 136).
27 *PDS Newsletter*, Berlin, August 1998.
28 The annual report of the German internal security body registered groups from these nationalities as among the main threats in Germany in 1997. See Bundesmijnisterium des Innern, *Verfassungsschutzbericht 1997*, Bonn, May 1998: 134. Countries like Britain do not publish reports.
29 *News from Austria*, 2 December 1998: 3. A survey carried out in 1996 revealed that 73 per cent of EU citizens surveyed thought it appropriate that the fight against drugs should be carried on by the EU rather than by national governments. There were majorities for EU decision-making on science and technology, foreign policy, the environment, political asylum rules, currency, immigration policy, the fight against unemployment and even defence. See *Standard Eurbarometer 46*, Autumn 1996.
30 *Das Parlament*, 20 November 1998: 1.
31 Dr Klaus Hänsch, 'Parliament needs greater strength', in Robert Morgan (ed.) *The Times Guide to the European Parliament*, June 1994. A *Standard Eurbarometer 46* poll in 1996 revealed that 54 per cent of EU citizens polled favoured a European government responsible to the European parliament.
32 *Daily Telegraph*, 17 December 1998.
33 Blair, 'There is a third way', *Daily Telegraph*, 23 July 1998.
34 *Das Parlament*, 8 December 1998: 1.
35 *Keesing's Record of World Events 1997*, 41563.
36 *News from Austria*, 16 December 1998: 2.
37 Luttwak, *Sunday Telegraph*, 3 January 1999.
38 Ambrose and Brinkley (1997: 169).
39 *SIPRI Yearbook 1995*.
40 *Daily Telegraph*, 17 October 1998.
41 *SIPRI Yearbook 1998*.
42 Marx and Engels (1967: 83).
43 *Daily Telegraph*, 12 December 1998; see also his interview with *Der Spiegel*, 14 December 1998.
44 *Daily Telegraph*, 7 October 1998.
45 *Granma International* (English edition), Havana, 21 February 1999. Castro announced new tough laws against 'trafficking of drugs and persons, pimping and robbery with violence'. Widespread, non-aggressive, begging was witnessed by the author in Cuba in February 1999.
46 *Granma International* (English edition), Havana, 21 February 1999.
47 *Keesing's Contemporary Archives, 1998*, 42006.
48 *Keesing's Contemporary Archives, 1998*, 42188.
49 *Keesing's Contemporary Archives, 1998*, 42188.
50 This is Jack London's formulation.

Chronology

1848	Marx and Engels publish *Communist Manifesto*. Year of revolutions ends in failure.
1849	An electric telegraph is installed between Paris and London. Crimean War (to 1856).
1856	Bessemer (UK) develops cheap production of steel.
1857	Indian mutiny against British fails.
1859	Charles Darwin's *The Origin of Species* published in London.
1861–5	American Civil War. Italy unified.
1864	First Workers' International founded in London.
1865	Abraham Lincoln assassinated.
1867	Marx's *Capital* published. Dominion of Canada established. Typewriter invented by Christopher L. Sholes (USA). Dynamite invented by Alfred Nobel (Sweden).
1868	Rapid Westernisation of Japan begins.
1869	Suez Canal formally opened. First transcontinental US railway.
1870	Franco-Prussian War leads to Paris Commune, which Marx describes as example of 'dictatorship of proletariat'. German Reich established. Papal infallibility becomes dogma of Catholic Church.
1875	German Social Democratic Party (SPD) set up.
1876	Karl Paul von Linde builds first practical refrigerator.
1878	First commercial telephone exchange opened in New Haven, CT.
1879	Pasteur discovers use of vaccines. Bebel's *Die Frau* published in Germany.
1880	In Vienna Freud and Breuer start collaboration using hypnosis.

1883	Death of Marx. Sickness and accident insurance begins in Germany.
1884–6	Widespread strikes in USA for eight-hour day. American Federation of Labor established. Dutch and Belgian Socialist parties formed.
1887	Daimler uses his internal combustion engine to produce a motor car.
1889	Second Socialist International established. Old-age pensions introduced in Germany. Social Democratic parties founded in Sweden and Austria.
1891	Erfurt Programme adopted by German Social Democrats.
1892	Socialist Party established in Italy. 'High tide of lynching' in USA when 235 Blacks publicly murdered.
1898	US–Spanish War over Cuba and Philippines. Zola's *J'Accuse* ... published in Paris.
1899	Bernstein's revisionist thesis, *The Preconditions for Socialism*, published. Anglo-Boer War, 1899–1902, British concentration camps. In USA DuBois' *The Philadelphia Negro. A Social Study* published.
1900	Labour Representation Committee (LRC) established in Britain. Boxer rebellion in China put down by European powers, USA and Japan. Commonwealth of Australia established.
1901	Trans-Siberian railway opened. Socialist Party of America set up.
1902	J.A. Hobson's *Imperialism* published in London.
1903	First successful aeroplane is launched by Wright brothers in USA.
1904	Russo-Japanese War leads to Russian defeat in 1905.
1905	Russian revolution fails. SFIO founded in France. Einstein formulates his special theory of relativity. Marie Curie becomes first woman professor at the Sorbonne. Lenin sets up Bolshevik party in London.
1906	Sweeping Liberal victory in Britain with Labour help, LRP becomes Labour Party. After mass demonstrations Iranian democratic constitution drawn up. Upton Sinclair's 'muck-raking' novel, *The Jungle*, appears in USA.

1907	Oil discovered in Iran exploited by Anglo-Persian Oil Company. Jack London's revolutionary novel, *The Iron Heel*, published in USA.
1908	'Young Turk' revolt in Turkey.
1909	Ford begins producing first cheap cars. Old-age pensions introduced by Liberals in Britain. National Association for the Advancement of Colored People (NAACP) set up.
1910	Mexican revolution.
1911	Chinese Republic established after overthrow of emperor. Federal income tax introduced in USA.
1912	SPD attracts vote of 34.8 per cent, and wins 27.7 per cent of the seats in the Reichstag, becoming the biggest parliamentary group.
1914	Outbreak of First World War which divides Socialists everywhere. Panama Canal opened.
1916	Easter Rising in Dublin against British.
1917	Russian revolution (February) followed by Bolshevik coup in October. Cheka established 20 December.
1918	Revolution in Germany establishes democratic German republic.
1919	End of World War with Versailles Treaty. 'Red Scare' in USA where widespread strikes take place.
1920	First commercial radio station, KDKA in Pittsburgh, established. Nineteenth Amendment to US constitution gives women the vote in presidental elections.
1921	Irish Free State (IFS) set up after guerrilla war with British. Chinese Communist Party established.
1922	Mussolini's 'March on Rome'. Civil war in IFS.
1924	First minority Labour government in Britain. Death of Lenin.
1925	Communist Party founded in Cuba.
1926	General strike in Britain, start of talking pictures. British Broadcasting Corporation (BBC) established.
1927	Anarchists Sacco and Vanzetti executed in USA.
1928	Women get right to vote in Britain on same terms as men. Alexander Fleming discovers penicillin; clinical use starts in 1940s.
1929	Wall Street crash brings world economic crisis. Stalin starts 'liquidation of Kulaks as a class'. Erich Maria

	Remarque's anti-war novel, *Ail Quiet On The Western Front*, published in Germany.
1930	The tape recorder using magnetised plastic tape is developed in Germany. Government of Hermann Müller resigns in Germany. Last SPD-led government till 1969.
1932	Swedish Social Democrats gain majority in parliament.
1933	Hitler's Nazis take over Germany and set up concentration camps. US President Roosevelt proclaims 'New Deal'. Machado dictatorship overthrown in Cuba.
1934	Civil war in Vienna, Socialists crushed.
1935	Saar returned to Germany. Nylon patented in USA. First television service in the world starts in Germany, 22 March.
1936	Popular Front electoral success in France and Spain. Outbreak of Spanish Civil War. Keynes publishes his *General Theory of Employment, Interest And Money*. Trotsky's *The Revolution Betrayed* is published. Regular TV broadcasts start in UK and Germany.
1937	Japan launches full-scale war on China.
1938	Show trial of Bukharin and others in Moscow. Austria annexed by Germany. Munich Agreement leads to dismemberment of Czechoslovakia.
1939	Hitler–Stalin Pact (August) outbreak of Second World War (September).Von Ohain's engine used in first jet to fly, He 178. Sikorsky constructs first helicopter designed for mass production.
1940	Fall of French Third Republic as Pétain agrees armistice with Germany. Labour joins coalition headed by Churchill. Battle of Britain. Trotsky assassinated in Mexico by Soviet agent.
1941	June, Nazi attack on Soviet Union. August, Anglo-Soviet invasion of Iran. September, SS start gassing prisoners in Auschwitz (Holocaust). December, Japan attacks USA.
1942	Fall of Singapore to Japanese. Beveridge Report (UK).
1943	German Sixth Army surrenders at Stalingrad.
1944	Hayek's *Road to Serfdom* published. D-Day landings, Germans launch V1 and V2 rockets against Britain. Edgar Snow's *Red Star Over China* published in New York.

1945	Roosevelt dies, Truman US president. End of war after atomic bombs dropped on Japan. British Labour victory. George Orwell's *Animal Farm* published. Forty-six nations meet in San Francisco to set up United Nations.
1946	Forced merger of SPD with Communists in Soviet Zone of Germany.
1947	Britain leaves Indian, Burma and Ceylon inaugurating postwar decolonisation.
1948	West Berlin blockaded by Soviets. Czech Communist coup. Stalin–Tito split. NATO established. State of Israel proclaimed.
1949	Two German states set up. Adenauer German chancellor. Mao takes over in China. Soviets become nuclear power. Orwell's *Nineteen Eighty-Four* published.
1950	Korean War. Diner's Club introduces first credit card. Leo Fender's 'Telecaster' first mass-produced electric guitar.
1951	Labour government defeated in Britain. Transcontinental TV in USA inaugurated.
1952	Slansky show trial in Prague. British Comet enters service as world's first all-jet airliner.
1953	Stalin dies. Revolt in East Germany.
1954	Elvis Presley makes his first recordings. French defeated in Vietnam.
1956	Khrushchev denounces Stalin. Hungarian revolution. Anglo-French Suez operation. Crosland's *The Future of Socialism* published.
1957	Rome Treaties, EEC established. Adenauer's greatest victory in West German election. Ghana first black African colony to gain independence. Soviets launch first artificial earth satellite. 'Youth culture' recognised in USA.
1958	Algerian revolt by French Right. De Gaulle takes over as President of Fifth Republic. EEC is established. Galbraith's *The Affluent Society* published in USA.
1959	Castro takes power in Cuba. Mass foreign tourism begins in Western Europe.
1961	Yuri Gagarin first human successfully launched into space (12 April). Berlin Wall (August). Sino-Soviet split. Solzhenitsyn's *One Day in the Life of Ivan Denisovich*

	published in Soviet Union. Bay of Pigs invasion of Cuba fails.
1960	US–Soviet missile crisis over Cuba.
1963	Gigantic march on Washington, DC, for black civil rights addressed by Martin Luther King. President Kennedy assassinated.
1964	Labour's victory under Wilson in British election. Khrushchev ousted. In USA Marcuse's *One Dimensional Man* published. Major US military involvement in Vietnam. US Civil Rights Act becomes law. Container ships introduced. 'Beatlemania' engulfs Britain.
1966	SPD joins CDU/CSU in grand coalition in West Germany. Cultural Revolution in China. US Air Force planes crash over Spain accidentally releasing four H-bombs.
1967	Arab–Israeli Six-Day War. Greek military coup. Christian Barnard performs first partially successful human heart transplant in South Africa. Che Guevara killed in Bolivia.
1968	Student revolts in Paris and elsewhere. Warsaw Pact forces invade Czechoslovakia and destroy 'Socialism with a human face'. Swedish Social Democrats win absolute majority of votes.
1969	Brandt elected West German chancellor. American moon landing.
1970	Kreisky wins absolute majority in Austrian elections.
1972	SPD achieved best electoral result since FRG established.
1973	Yom Kippur War, followed by oil crisis. UK, Ireland, Denmark join EEC/EC. Solzhenitsyn's *Gulag Archipelago* published in Paris. Allende coalition overthrown by Pinochet in Chile.
1974	Fall of dictatorship in Portugal and Greece.
1975	End of Vietnam War. First personal computer introduced in USA.
1976	End of dictatorship in Spain. Swedish Social Democrats defeated. Mao dies. Carrillo completes his *'Eurocommunism' and the State*.
1979	Thatcher defeats Labour in Britain. Soviet invasion of Afghanistan. Revolution in Iran. Second oil crisis.

1980   Reagan inaugurated US president (in office to 1988).
          Polish unrest. Fax machines and mobile phones make
          their appearance.
1981   Mitterrand elected French president. Greece joins
          EEC/EC.
1982   Schmidt falls and is replaced by Kohl (CDU). Falklands
          War. PSOE wins election in Spain. Compact disc intro-
          duced. Aids disease publicised.
1983   Kohl wins West German election. Thatcher re-elected.
          Apple introduces the 'mouse' to personal computers.
1985   Gorbachev elected CPSU leader.
1986   Spain and Portugal join EEC/EC. Chernobyl nuclear
          explosion.
1989   Fall of Honecker in GDR, opening of Berlin Wall. Bush
          US president (to 1993).
1990   GDR votes for German reunification from 3 October.
          Kohl wins first election of reunited Germany. Mandela
          released from prison.
1991   Gorbachev overthrown, end of Soviet Union. Gulf War.
          Maastricht Treaty negotiated.
1992   Clinton (Democrat) wins US election, inaugurated presi-
          dent (1993).
1994   Mandela elected South African president.
1995   Austria, Finland and Sweden join EU.
1996   USA tightens blockade of Cuba.
1997   Blair wins British election, PS under Jospin wins French
          election.
1998   Pope visits Cuba. SPD wins election in Germany.
1999   Single currency, Euro, introduced by eleven states of the
          EU.

Bibliography

General

Ambrose, Stephen E. and Douglas G. Brinkley (1997) *Rise to Globalism: American Foreign Policy Since 1938*, London.

Andics, Hellmut (1968) *50 Jahre Unseres Lebens. Österreichs Schicksal seit 1918*, Vienna.

Avril, Pierre (1969) *Politics in France*, Harmondsworth.

Bark, Dennis L. and David R. Gress (1993) *A History Of West Germany*, 2 vols, Cambridge, MA.

Benson, Frederick R. (1968) *Writers in Arms*, London.

Berchtold, Klaus (ed.) (1967) *Österreichische Parteiprogramme 1868–1966*, Munich.

Blight, James G. and Peter Kornbluh (1998) *Politics of Illusion, The Bay of Pigs Invasion Revisited*, Boulder, CO.

Blondel, Jean and E. Drexel Godfrey Jr (1968) *The Government of France*, London.

Boyce, D.G. (1972) *Englishmen and Irish Troubles*, London.

Buchanan, Tom (1997) *Britain and the Spanish Civil War*, Cambridge.

Butler, David (1995) *British General Elections Since 1945*, Oxford.

Butler, David and Dennis Kavanagh (1997) *The British General Election of 1997*, London.

Carsten, F.L. (1982) *The Rise of Fascism*, London.

Clarke, Thomas and Christos Pitelis (1995) *The Political Economy of Privatization*, London.

Cobban, Alfred (1968) *A History of Modern France, vol. 3, 1871–1962*, Harmondsworth.

Conrad, Will C., Kathleen Wilson and Dale Wilson (1964) *The Milwaukee Journal. The First Eighty Years*, Madison.

Cowling, David (ed.) (1988) *America. The '88 Vote. An ITN Factbook*, London.

Coxall, Bill and Lynton Robins (1998) *British Politics Since the War*, London.

Cross, Tim (1988) *The Lost Voices of World War*, London.

Crossman, Richard (ed.) (1950) *The God That Failed*, London.

Department of Defense (1985) *Black Americans in Defense of our Nation*, Washington, DC.

Derbyshire, Ian (1986) *Politics in France from Giscard to Mitterrand*, London.

Evans, Eric J. (1997) *Thatcher and Thatcherism*, London.

FitzGibbon, Louis (1971) *Katyn Massacre. A Searing Indictment of the Shameful Concealment of Mass Murder*, London.

Frazier, Robert (1991) *Anglo-American Relations with Greece. The Coming of the Cold War 1942–47*, London.

Galbraith, John Kenneth (1977) *The Age of Uncertainty*, London.

Gilbert, Martin (1989) *Second World War*, London.

Ginsborg, Paul (1989) *A History of Contemporary Italy. Society And Politics 1943–1988*, London.

Gundle, Stephen and Simon Parker (eds) (1996) *The New Italian Republic*, London.

Hancock, M. Donald et al. (1998) *Politics in Western Europe*, London.

Henig, Stanley (1997) *The Uniting of Europe. From Discord to Concord*, London.

Hewison, Robert (1995) *Culture and Consensus England. Art and Politics since 1940*, London.

Heywood, Paul (1995) *The Government and Politics of Spain*, London.

Hogg, Quintin (1947) *The Case for Conservatism*, London.

Howe, Geoffrey (1994) *Conflict of Loyalty*, London.

Hülsberg, Werner (1988) *The German Greens. A Social and Political Profile*, London.

Hutton, Will (1995) *The State We're In*, London.

Irving, R.E.M. (1979) *The Christian Democratic Parties of Western Europe*, London.

Kitchen, Martin (1980) *The Coming of Austrian Fascism*, London.

Krout, John A. (1973) *The United States Since 1865*, New York.

Leifer, Michael (1996) *Dictionary of Modern Politics of Southeast Asia*, London.

Little, Douglas (1985) *Malevolent Neutrality. The United States, Great Britain, and the Origins of the Spanish Civil War*, Ithaca.

Lovenduski, Joni (1986) *Women and European Politics*, Brighton.

Luther, Richard and Peter Pulzer (1998) *Austria 1945–95*, Aldershot.

McAllister, Richard (1997) *From EC to EU. An Historical and Political Survey*, London.

Maravall, Jose (1982) *The Transition to Democracy in Spain*, London.

Marquand, David (1991) *The Progressive Dilemma. From Lloyd George to Kinnock*, London.

Miles, Lee (ed.) (1996) *The EU and the Nordic Countries*, London.

Mintzel, Alf and Heinrich Oberreuter (eds) (1990) *Parteien in der Bundesrepublik Deutschland*, Bonn.
Parkinson, Roger (1977) *The Encyclopaedia of Modern War*, New York.
Perryman, Mark (ed.) (1996) *The Blair Agenda*, London.
Pincher, Chapman (1986) *Their Trade Is Treachery*, London.
Pollard, Sidney (1997) *The International Economy since 1945*, London.
Read, Anthony and David Fisher (1988) *The Deadly Embrace: Hitler, Stalin and the Nazi-Soviet Pact 1939–1941*, London.
Royal Danish Foreign Ministry (1961) *Denmark*, Copenhagen.
Royle, Trevor (1987) *War Report*, Edinburgh.
Salmon, Keith (1995) *The Modern Spanish Economy*, 2nd edition, London.
Seale, Patrick and Maureen McConville (1968) *French Revolution 1968*, London.
Shipman, David (1982) *The Story of Cinema, Volume II*, London.
Smith, Denis Mack (1997) *Modern Italy. A Political History*, New Haven, CT.
Steed, Philip John (1985) *The Police in Britain*, New York.
Sully, Melanie A. (1981) *Political Parties and Elections in Austria*, London.
Thomas, Hugh (1965) *The Spanish Civil War*, Harmondsworth.
Urwin, D.W. (1991) *Western Europe Since 1945. A Short Political History*, London.
Wallich, Henry C. (1955) *Mainsprings of the German Revival*, New Haven, CT.
Wheen, Francis (1985) *Television. A History*, London.
Young, John W. (1991) *Cold War Europe 1945–1989. A Political History*, London.

Articles

Fitzmaurice, John (1996) 'The Austrian General Election of 17 December 1995', *German Politics*, vol. 5, no. 2, August.
Luther, Kurt Richard (1995) 'Austria in Light of the 1994 Elections', *German Politics*, vol. 4, no. 1, April.
Madeley, John (1998) 'The Politics of Embarrassment: Norway's 1997 Election', *West European Politics*, vol. 21, no. 2, April.
Müller, Wolfgang C. (1992) 'The Catch-all Party Thesis and the Austrian Social Democrats', *German Politics*, vol. 1, no. 2, August.

Biographies

Anderson, Jon Lee (1997) *Che Guerra. A Revolutionary Life*, London.
Ascherson, Neal (1982) Introduction to *The Book of Lech Walesa*, London.
Beckett, Francis (1997) *Clem Attlee*, London.
Brandt, Willy (1992) *My Life in Politics*, New York.
Brown, Archie (1996) *The Gorbachev Factor*, Oxford.

Callaghan, James (1987) *Time and Chance*, London.

Campbell, John (1993) *Edward Heath. A Biography*, London.

Castanede, Jorge (1997) *Companero. The Life and Death of Che Guevara*, London.

Cole, Alistair (1997) *François Mitterrand*, London.

Cross, Colin (1966) *Philip Snowden*, London.

Drower, George (1994) *Kinnock*, London.

Edinger, Lewis J. (1965) *Kurt Schumacher*, Stanford, CA.

Foot, Michael (1975) *Aneurin Bevan*, London.

Gilbert, Martin (1976) *Winston Spencer Churchill, vol. V, 1922–1939*, London.

Gorbachev, Mikhail (1997) *Memoirs*, London.

Healey, Denis (1989) *The Time of my Life*, London.

Hollis, Patricia (1997) *Jennie Lee. A Life*, London.

Howe, Geoffrey (1994) *Conflict of Loyalty*, London.

Hyde, Douglas (1951) *I Believed. The Autobiography of a Former Communist*, London.

Jenkins, Roy (1948) *Mr Attlee. An Interim Biography*, London.

Jones, Mervyn (1995) *Michael Foot*, London.

Kavanagh, Dennis (ed.) (1998) *Dictionary of Political Biography*, Oxford.

Kerstein, Edward S. (1966) *Milwaukee's All-American Mayor: Portrait of Daniel Webster Hoan*, Englewood Cliffs, NJ.

Lacouture, Jean (1990) *De Gaulle. The Rebel 1890–1944*, London.

Lawrence, Alan (1998) *China under Communism*, London.

McCauley, Martin (1998) *Gorbachev*, London.

Marquand, David (1977) *Ramsay MacDonald*, London.

Maser, Werner (1990) *Friedrich Ebert. Der erste deutsche Reichspräsident*, Frankfurt/Berlin.

Owen, David (1992) *Time to Declare*, London.

Pimlott, Ben (ed.) (1986) *The Political Diary of Hugh Dalton, 1918–40, 1945–60*, London.

—— (1996) *The Queen. A Biography of Elizabeth II*, London.

Ponting, Clive (1995) *Churchill*, London.

Rentoul, John (1996) *Tony Blair*, London.

Scammell, Michael (1986) *Solzhenitsyn*, London.

Scholz, Günther (1988) *Kurt Schumacher*, Düsseldorf.

Schwarz, Hans-Peter (1986) *Adenauer. Der Aufstieg: 1876–1952*, Stuttgart.

Seebacher-Brandt, Brigitte (1984) *Ollenhauer Biedermann und Patriot*, Berlin.

—— (1988) *Bebel Künder und Kärner im Kaiserreich*, Berlin/Bonn.

Shawcross, William (1990) *Dubcek and Czechoslovakia, 1918–1990*, London.

Sudoplatov, Pavel (1994) *Special Tasks. The Memoirs of an Unwanted Witness. A Soviet Spymaster*, New York.

Thatcher, Margaret (1995) *The Path to Power*, London.

Winstone, Ruth (ed.) (1995) *The Benn Diaries*, London.
Wolf, Markus (1998) *Spionagechef im geheimen Krieg*, Munich.
Wright, Peter (1987) *Spy Catcher. The Candid Autobiography of a Senior Intelligence Officer*, New York.
Ziegler, Philip (1995) *Wilson. The Authorised Life*, London.

Communist systems and Eastern Europe

Andrew, Christopher and Oleg Gordievsky (1990) *KGB. The Inside Story*, New York.
Brogan, Patrick (1990) *Eastern Europe: The 50 Years War, 1939–89*, London.
Bundesministerium für gesamtdeutsche Fragen (1969) *A bis Z. Ein Taschen- und Nachschlagebuch über den anderen Teil Deutschlands*, Bonn.
Carrillo, Santiago (1977) *'Eurocommunism' and the State*, London.
Childs, David (1988) *The GDR. Moscow's German Ally*, London.
Childs, David and Richard Popplewell (1996) *The Stasi: The East German Intelligence and Security System*, London.
Clissold, Stephen (ed.) (1966) *A Short History of Yugoslavia*, London.
Crampton, J.R. (1997) *Eastern Europe in the Twentieth Century and After*, London.
Furtak, Robert (1986) *The Political Systems of the Socialist States*, Brighton.
Gelb, Norman (1986) *The Berlin Wall*, London.
Grimm, Tilmann (ed.) (1967) *Das Rote Buch. Worte des Vorsitzenden Mao Tse-tung*, Frankfurt/Hamburg.
Hertle, Hans-Hermann (1996) *Chronik des Mauerfalls*, Berlin.
Klugmann, James (1951) *From Trotsky to Tito*, London.
Knechtel, Rüdiger and Jürgen Fiedler (1992) *Stalins DDR. Berichte politisch Verfolgter*, Leipzig.
Lawrence, Alan (1998) *China under Communism*, London.
Lomax, Bill (1976) *Hungary 1956*, London.
Ludz, Peter Christian (1979) *DDR Handbuch*, Bonn.
McCauley, Martin (1981) *The Soviet Union Since 1917*, London.
Mackerras, Colin (1998) *China in Transition, 1900–1949*, Harlow.
Marshall, Peter (1988) *Cuba Libre. Breaking the Chains?*, London.
Marx, Karl and Friedrich Engels (1967) *The Communist Manifesto*, with an introduction by A.J.P. Taylor, Harmondsworth.
Mills, C. Wright (ed.) (1982) *The Marxists*, New York.
Moise, Edwin E. (1994) *Modern China. A History*, Harlow.
Naimark, Norman and Leonard Gibianski (1998) *The Establishment of Communist Regimes in Eastern Europe, 1944–1949*, Oxford.
Pike, David (1992) *The Politics of Culture in Soviet-Occupied Germany 1945–1949*, Stanford, CA.
Roberts, Geoffrey (1999) *The Soviet Union in World Politics*, London.

Schabowski, Günter (1990) *Das Politbüro*, Reinbek bei Hamburg.

Shawcross, William (1990) *Dubcek and Czechoslovakia, 1918–1990*, London.

Sutton, A.C. (1973) *Western Technology and Soviet Economic Developments, vol. 3, 1945–65*, Stanford, CA.

Swain, Geoffrey and Nigel Swain (1993) *Eastern Europe Since 1945*, London.

Weber, Hermann (1991) *DDR Grundriß der Geschichte 1954–1990*, Hanover.

Weitz, Eric D. (1997) *Creating German Communism, 1890–1990*, Princeton, NJ.

Westwood, J.N. (1993) *Endurance and Endeavour. Russian History 1812–1992*, London.

Winberg, Chai (ed.) (1968) *Essential Works of Chinese Communism*, New York.

Zauberman, A. (1964) *Industrial Progress in Poland, Czechoslovakia and Eastern Germany 1937–1962*, London.

Labour/Communist movements and the New Left

Ali, Tariq and Susan Watkins (1998) *1968: Marching in the Streets*, London.

Anderson, P. and P. Camiller (eds) (19 *Mapping the West European Left*, London.

Barnes, Samuel H. (1967) *Party Democracy: Politics in the Italian Socialist Federation*, New Haven, CT.

Beck, Elmer A. (1982a) *The Sewer Socialists, vol. I, The Socialist Trinity of the Party, the Unions and the Press*, Fennimore, WI.

—— (1982b) *The Sewer Socialists, vol. II, The Nineteen-twenties and Nineteen-thirties*, Fennimore, WI.

Bell, Daniel (1967) *Marxian Socialism in the United States*, Princeton, NJ.

Bell, D.S. and Byron Criddle (1988) *The French Socialist Party. The Emergence of a Party of Government*, Oxford.

Blackmer, L.M. and Sidney Tarrow (eds) (1975) *Communism in Italy and France*, Princeton, NJ.

Branson, Noreen (1985) *History of the Communist Party of Great Britain, 1927–41*, London.

Braunthal, Gerard (1983) *The West German Social Democrats, 1969–1982. Profile of a Party in Power*, Boulder, CO.

Bull, Martin and Paul Heywood (eds) (1994) *West European Communist Parties after the Revolutions of 1989*, New York.

Castles, Francis G. (1979) *The Social Democratic Image of Society*, London.

Caute, David (1966) *The Left in Europe since 1789*, London.

Childs, David (1966) *From Schumacher to Brandt. The Story of German Socialism 1945–65*, Oxford.

—— (ed.) (1980) *The Changing Face of Western Communism*, London.

Chun Lin (1993) *The British New Left*, Edinburgh.

Claudin, Fernando (1978) *Eurocommunism and Socialism*, London.

Crew, Ivor and Anthony King (1995) *SDP. The Birth, Life and Death of the Social Democratic Party*, Oxford.

Darke, Bob (1952) *The Communist Technique in Britain*, Harmondsworth.

De Grand, Alexander (1989) *The Italian Left in the 20th Century*, Bloomington and Indianapolis.

Elvander, Nils (1979) *Scandinavian Social Democracy: Its Strengths and Weaknesses*, Uppsala.

Foot, Paul (1968) *The Politics of Harold Wilson*, Harmondsworth.

Fletcher, Roger (ed.) (1987) *Bernstein to Brandt*, London.

Fraser, Ronald (ed.) (1988) *1968: An International Oral History*, New York.

Gillespie, Richard (1989) *The Spanish Socialist Party. A History of Factionalism*, Oxford.

Graham, Helen (1991) *Socialism and War. The Spanish Socialist Party in Power and Crisis, 1936–39*, Cambridge.

Heywood, Paul (1990) *Marxism and the Failure of Organised Socialism in Spain 1879–1936*, Oxford.

Horn, Gerd-Rainer (1997) *European Socialists Respond to Fascism*, London.

Johnson, R.W. (1981) *The Long March of the French Left*, Manchester.

Joll, James (1955) *The Second International 1889–1914*, London.

Kendall, Walter (1975) *The European Labour Movement*, London.

Lichtheim, George (1975) *A Short History of Socialism*, London.

Machin, Howard (ed.) (1983) *National Communism in Western Europe*, London.

McLellan, David (1971) *The Thought of Karl Marx*.

Maravall, Jose (1978) *Dictatorship and Political Dissent. Workers and Students in Franco's Spain*, London.

Mortimer, Edward (1984) *The Rise of the French Communist Party 1920–47*.

Noland, Aaron (1970) *The Founding of the French Socialist Party (1893–1905)*, New York.

Nugent, Neill and David Lowe (1982) *The Left in France*, London.

Oglesby, Carl (1969) *The New Left Reader*, New York.

Ollman, Bertell (1998) *Market Socialism*, London.

Osterroth, Franz and Dieter Schuster (1978) *Chronik der deutschen Sozialdemokratie*, 3 vols, Berlin/Bonn.

Padgett, Stephen and W.E. Paterson (1991) *A History of Social Democracy in Post-war Europe*, London.

Paterson, W.E. and A.H. Thomas (eds) (1986) *The Future of Social Democracy: Problems and Prospects of Social Democratic Parties in Western Europe*, Oxford.

Pierson, Christopher (1996) *Socialism after Communism. The New Market Socialism*, London.

Ramsay, Robin (1998) *Prawn Cocktail Party. The Hidden Power Behind New Labour*, London.

Sassoon, Donald (1996) *One Hundred Years of Socialism: The West European Left in the Twentieth Century*, London.

Schapiro, Leonard (1970) *The Communist Party of the Soviet Union*, London.

Scharf, F. (1991) *Crisis and Choice in Swedish Social Democracy*, Ithaca, NY.

Seyd, Patrick (1987) *The Rise and Fall of the Labour Left*, London.

Shipley, Peter (1976) *Revolutionaries in Modern Britain*, London.

Socialist Union (1956) *Twentieth Century Socialism*, London.

Thompson, Willie (1992) *The Good Old Cause. British Communism 1920–1991*, London.

Turner, Lowell (1998) *Fighting for Partnership. Labour and Politics in Unified Germany*, Ithaca, NY.

Urban, Joan Barth (1986) *Moscow and the Italian Communist Party*, London.

Wilde, Lawrence (1994) *Modern European Socialism*, Aldershot.

Wilson, Frank L. (1971) *The French Democratic Left, 1963–1969*, Stanford, CA.

Wright, Tony (1996) *Socialisms Old and New*, London.

Name index

Subject index